STAYING AI

MW00699255

ROAD

THE ART OF DRIVER SITUATIONAL AWARENESS

Karl Schlimm

Chandler, AZ

Copyright © 2017 by Karl A. Schlimm.

All rights reserved. No part of this publication may be reproduced, distributed, or transmitted in any form or by any means, including photocopying, recording, or other electronic or mechanical methods, without the prior written permission of the publisher, except in the case of brief quotations embodied in critical reviews and certain other noncommercial uses permitted by copyright law. For permission requests, or for information about special discounts available for bulk purchases, sales promotions, fund-raising and educational needs, write to the publisher at the address below, or you may contact the publisher at the phone number listed.

First Published July 2017

ISBN 9781973335573

E-book version also available on Amazon:
ASIN B07432DB5Q

Karl A. Schlimm, Publisher

(480) 239-8239

Dedicated to: My wife Rene, son Nick, and my mother Janice. They have patiently heard me say I am two weeks away from publishing this book for the past two years. I am thankful for their encouragement and assistance in my writing side venture.

TABLE OF CONTENTS

FROM THE AUTHOR

Hello, and thank you for purchasing my book! My name is Karl Schlimm. I am a former U.S. Air Force Fighter Pilot, author, and aviation consultant in areas requiring a high level of situational awareness. I personally have over 8000 adrenaline-filled flight hours and three decades of experience in a wide range of aircraft including the supersonic F-16 "Fighting Falcon" fighter jet, the supersonic T-38 Talon jet trainer, the T-37 and Siai-Marchetti S211 subsonic jet trainers, the OV-10, the Unlimited Class Aerobatic Extra 300L, the Boeing 767-300 Heavy, Boeing 757 and about two dozen other aircraft. In the complex, hazardous environments in which I have routinely flown, not only as a fighter jet instructor and formation airshow pilot, but also as a commercial pilot, I have become well-versed in the art of situational awareness, or "SA," as a foundation for making life-saving decisions. As an experienced driver, I apply the principles of SA directly to my driving to enhance safety as well as my enjoyment of driving.

PREFACE

Teerawut Masawat/123RF

The information presented in *Staying Alive on the Road: The Art of Driver Situational Awareness* is, as the title implies, specifically oriented to automobile drivers. However, the fundamental principles of situational awareness outlined in the following pages apply equally as well to the operation of automobiles, airplanes, boats, even snowmobiles. In fact, these principles can enhance your safety and awareness in almost any complex human activity where not paying attention to what you are doing and to your surroundings can be deadly. This book is for all drivers and operators, from beginner to experienced. Below are just some of the valuable lessons that you will learn in *Staying Alive on The Road:*

1. The principles of **situational awareness**, or "**SA**," which can be applied to any activity.

2. How to gain and maintain a high level of SA, and how good driving decisions—to keep you alive—cannot be made without it.

3. The three forms of distraction—visual, manual, and cognitive—and why, while texting is one of the most dangerous activities you can perform when driving, even talking on a cell phone (for example) can be dangerous.

4. All of the elements of the driving "domain" to include you, your vehicle, the road, traffic, signs, debris, weather, and other elements and hazards that make this domain so complex.

5. Your driving cognitive (mental) model, and how it is an incomplete picture of the real world, making what you pay attention to on the road all the more important.

6. Why it is so important for you to have high SA before you need it; because once you need it, it is often too late to build SA to safe levels to avoid a crash.

7. How to effectively scan visually, given the limits of human vision; how to choose the appropriate driving eyewear to enhance visual scanning and acuity; and the importance of using all of your senses, not just vision, to maintain high SA.

8. Goal awareness, how your goals determine what you pay most attention to; and why it is critical to make the goal of safe driving more important than the goal of getting somewhere at any given moment.

9. Self-awareness, or an awareness of your experience level in current driving conditions, and also an awareness of your physical and mental state, to include your behavioral disposition and propensity for road rage (and how to deal with other drivers' road rage).

10. Vehicle awareness; or knowing your car's maintenance and systems' status.

11. How to "be one" with your vehicle, by learning to set up your seat, mirrors and lights appropriately, and by being aware of your vehicle's field-of-view limitations (blind spots).

12. Maneuvering awareness; or being aware of how to maneuver within your limitations, and your vehicle's limitations, so that you can avoid losing control of your vehicle; and how to react safely in a crisis such as a tire blowout or failed brakes.

13. Available automobile safety technology to help keep you alive; and the limitations of vehicle user-interactive technology and distractions associated with it.

14. Limitations of human spatial awareness, and why you cannot reliably keep your place on the road and avoid unanticipated hazards when your attention is somewhere else.

15. How to assess traffic properly, and why it is important to know who is around and behind you in the present, where that traffic will be in the near future…and where you would go if you had to maneuver quickly to avoid a crash, or to pull over.

16. Temporal awareness; or being able to accurately determine how your environment, including traffic, will change in the near future…an essential skill to have in order to safely pass, merge, or turn into traffic while avoiding a collision.

17. The dangers of night driving and how to cope.

18. The dangers of complacency and also high task workload; how to prioritize tasks; and the myth of multitasking.

19. The importance of leaving yourself an "out," and of leaving the other driver an "out" as well.

Staying Alive on the Road: The Art of Driver Situational Awareness is more of a study of the principles of situational awareness applied to routine driving than a step-by-step how-to book. I hope it will save some lives. I've used a little creative license in that many aviation analogies are included, which hopefully will enhance your understanding of the concepts of situational awareness. I have included a graphic depiction of driver situational awareness on the cover and at the beginning of Chapter Five. It serves as a reference for you to study as you read and reread the information contained here. As you read this guide, think about how these principles apply to your own driving situation given your experience, driving habits, and local traffic and road conditions. As you drive, take your time incorporating these principles. Change your habits at a pace you can handle safely. Although my examples specifically address left-hand-drive vehicles in right-side driving situations (as in the U.S.), these principles, of course, apply to all drivers, regardless of location of steering wheel or on which side of the road you drive. Since this guide is for all operators, regardless of technical background, I have not simplified the explanation of the principles of SA, because I know you are up for the challenge!

A Word of Caution (and Disclaimer): Please use the concepts in this book for your benefit. However, nothing contained in this guide replaces or supersedes local or national driving laws. You are completely responsible for complying with those driving laws and for driving and allocating your attention within your own personal abilities and limitations. Please use common sense when driving and when directing your attention! As you will see, driving with low situational awareness can kill you. However, approaching SA principles too rigidly while driving can cause fixation of attention or misallocation of attention at just the wrong time, and that can be deadly as well. I cannot be responsible for your actions as a driver that might result in damage to personal property, injury or death. Please use this guide to hone your SA skills, but always allocate your attention wisely given your specific driving conditions, and please always act conservatively. Common sense and sound judgment always apply.

You only gain the ability to have a high level of situational awareness—or "high SA"—by understanding it and by practicing it. If you always drive distracted, you will never become a better driver. Whether you have been driving for one month or several decades, this guide can change the way you think and act while driving and make you a much safer driver. I learned the principles of SA while flying aircraft and have applied them to my daily driving for over three-and-a-half decades. I am now sharing these principles with you so that, after reading this guide, you can apply the principles of SA to your daily driving, as well as to any other activity in your life.

CHAPTER ONE: INTRODUCTION TO SITUATIONAL AWARENESS

Michael Rosskothen /123RF

The Origin and Nature of Situational Awareness: Although the principles of situational awareness have been around for centuries, the concepts of SA in aviation originated during World War I, when tacticians like Fighter Ace Oswald Boelcke began formalizing the traits needed for aviators to survive while operating their aircraft during wartime. Today, military and civilian pilots fly in an environment which has become increasingly complex and dynamic. A pilot may face the challenge at any time of having to make a time-critical life or death decision.

To make good decisions, pilots must undoubtedly rely upon their aviation knowledge and flying experience. However, they must also have an accurate "real-time" visualization, or "mental model," of a complex set of elements in their flying environment, also known as a flying "domain," to include their own capabilities, personal limitations and physical state, the status of their aircraft's systems and fuel state, their location, other aircraft in the vicinity, and hazards including terrain, and weather.

The Dynamic Nature of SA: These elements in the aviation environment, or domain, are oftentimes very dynamic or fleeting in nature, for two reasons: First, the nature of these elements changes in time; weather gets worse over time, systems fail in time, etc. Second, pilots and their vehicles move, usually very rapidly, through the environment into changing conditions; pilots fly into changing air traffic or transition from the high-altitude environment to the landing environment. Indeed, elements that make up any vehicle operator's domain, whether it be the domain of flying, driving, sailing, or any other, change both in time, and with location relative to the operator and vehicle.

Pilots cannot possibly assimilate all the data in their changing environment; no operator in a complex environment can. The driving environment in its simplest condition is still a complex environment. Pilots, drivers, indeed all operators of a machine or system, must therefore prioritize attention to only the most important information in their environment to suit their most pressing objectives.

A pilot's goals, or "objectives," can range from basic navigation, to approaching an airport for landing, even responding to an emergency. Perceiving, comprehending and predicting the future state of all this information or sensory data to form a mental model (discussed later) of one's environment is the essence of situational awareness, or "SA." The art of having a high level of SA, or "high SA," can be practiced and perfected. It is the foundation of effective decision making. Having low situational awareness, or "low SA," means potentially making a bad decision—even making no decision—either of which can be deadly. Not surprisingly, this is true when driving on the road.

The Paradox of Experience: When we think of the term *"experience,"* we generally think, simply, of the hours spent doing something. A 5000-hour pilot, driver—any other operator—has more experience than a 500-hour operator. On the other hand, when we think of the phrase *"being experienced,"* we assume a certain level of expertise or proficiency at one's craft. However, whether the high-time operator is any better at his or her craft than an operator who has less time is an entirely different matter.

Experience, at least in terms of hours spent behind the controls of an aircraft, automobile, or other vehicle, does not guarantee a similar level of "being experienced" or being "really good" at a task. We naturally expect an operator to get better at what he or she does with more hours spent at an activity. Perhaps this is a valid general assumption. Let's face it though; some of us can spend a lifetime doing something and never become good at it. Yes, high time pilots are better on average than low time pilots. After all, pilot training is closely regulated, and pilots must frequently pass tough initial and recurrent proficiency check flights or simulator sessions to keep flying.

Although drivers have every opportunity to get better at the art of driving the more time spent behind the wheel, there is conspicuously no comparable level of training or regulatory oversight in driving proficiency as there is in flying. In other words, drivers can basically remain bad at driving forever, and no one is there to call them out on it. As a driver, you can literally "slip through the cracks." When is the last time you had to take a driving proficiency check?

It is never too late to become a better driver. Learning the principles of SA above and beyond what was ever taught in your driver's education program can not only make you a safer driver, but can, for the driving enthusiast or purist, make driving more enjoyable as well.

CHAPTER TWO: MOTOR VEHICLE CRASH STATISTICS

Evgenii Naumov/123RF

A look at crash statistics can shed light not only on the most common causes of crashes but also on the myriad hazards that drivers perhaps unwittingly deal with every day. The 2017 U.S. Department of Transportation National Highway Traffic Safety Administration (NHTSA) study indicated that 37,133 motor vehicle-related fatalities occurred in the U.S. in 2017, a 1.8% decrease from 2016 but still a 5.8% increase from 2015. Of note, almost half of passenger vehicle occupants killed in 2017 were not restrained, so many of those fatalities could undoubtedly have been avoided if more vehicle occupants had buckled up. Fatality statistics are misleading, as seventy times as many people were injured, many permanently disabled, as were killed. Over 90% of vehicle crashes in the survey were due to human error, as is typically true in most similar activities. Alcohol impairment was involved in a third of accidents; another third of accidents in the study were speeding related. As we will see, however, these factors do not happen in isolation. Driving sober, well-rested and at the speed limit merely enables a driver to better contend with the many hazards in the driving environment; it does not eliminate them.

The Cause of Crashes: The NHTSA conducted a National Motor Vehicle Crash Causation Survey (NMVCCS) for report to Congress in 2008. A major reason for conducting this survey was to clarify the events leading up to a crash so that needless fatalities could be avoided in the future. Although the report is somewhat dated, the lessons learned are timeless.

The NMVCCS reported some very revealing statistics regarding 5471 crashes which occurred over a 2 ½ year period from July 2005 to December 2007. An analysis of pre-crash events—specifically, the event immediately preceding the crash—revealed the following data: 31% of accidents occurred while the driver was turning or crossing intersections, 22% of drivers ran off the edge of road, 11% of drivers failed to stay in the proper lane, 12% of drivers were stopped, and 9% of drivers lost control prior to the crash. So, a full third of accidents were attributable to turning or crossing intersections, which indicates just how dangerous this activity is— and, as we'll see, why it is important for you to have high situational awareness when doing it. And, combining the percentage of drivers who ran off the road and drivers who failed to stay in their lane, a full third of drivers basically failed to keep their cars safely within the lane boundaries of the road. Intuitively, distraction—and hence low SA—was probably a major factor in many of these accidents. The NMVCCS also reported the "critical reason" for crashes in the following categories:

The Driver: About 41% of crashes attributable to the driver were caused by recognition errors due to driver inattention, distractions inside and outside the vehicle, and inadequate or improper surveillance (attention and visual scanning). In fact, 18% of all accidents involved drivers engaging in at least one non-driving activity, such as a conversation with another passenger or talking on a cell phone; 34% of crashes were due to decision errors such as driving aggressively or too fast. Driving performance errors like overcompensation (overcorrecting or swerving while maneuvering) and improper directional control leading to loss of control comprised 10% of crashes. Fatigued drivers were twice as likely to make these performance errors.

The Vehicle: Tire or wheel failure was the most significant factor when the vehicle was attributable, followed by braking system failure.

The Roadway and Atmospheric Conditions: Where the critical reason was attributed to the roadway (road design, road signage, traffic control, or sight distance, which is the length of roadway visible to the driver) or atmospheric (weather) conditions, a slick road surface due to ice or debris was the most prevalent cause, followed by obstructions to driver vision. Of note, 30% of these crashes involved a single vehicle.

Driving seems so easy that we oftentimes take the task for granted. But, to suggest just how complicated driving consistently safely is, consider that the NMVCCS data spanned a staggering 600 variables or factors related to drivers, vehicles, roadway, and environment. From that, one could easily infer that maintaining situational awareness in any driving situation involves myriad factors depending on what your driving priorities are, and how complex your particular driving environment is. Driving may seem safe, perhaps because you have continually escaped serious harm while texting, talking, or engaging in other driving distractions, but this fact may not be indicative of just how narrow your margin of safety is when distracted. You may not realize just how close you have repeatedly come to injuring or killing yourself, a passenger or someone else.

The Accident Causal Chain ("Swiss Cheese" Model): Sometimes the cause of a car crash is cut and dry, caused by one simple act of omission or negligence. Texting while driving is an example of that. It does not matter whether you are on top of your game, rested and refreshed and feeling like King Kong on the road. If you text and drive, or do anything of similar distraction such as looking down for more than a second or two at a map display, you are, in that moment, negligent in your driving duties. It does not matter how many fancy displays and gadgets your automobile has, the task of driving remains simple; keep your eyes on the road, remain focused on the task of driving and be ready for anything. Even if you have a self-driving mode (autopilot) in your vehicle, you are still responsible for monitoring its status and performance, as any pilot will tell you. You must be prepared to take over quickly. When on the road and at the wheel, never let your guard down. You are the pilot-in-command, the captain of the ship. And you have a responsibility for saving lives. I cannot count how many times I have seen drivers on the highway, changing lanes, coming to a stop at an intersection – and looking down at their cell phone.

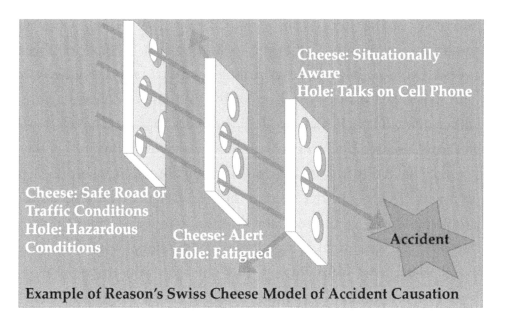

Example of Reason's Swiss Cheese Model of Accident Causation

Many times, the cause of an accident is not clear cut. Instead, it is sometimes caused by numerous seemingly insignificant acts of omission, negligence or carelessness that add up to an accident. The "Swiss Cheese" Model of Accident Causation was proposed by Dante Orlandella and Edward T. Reason. The figure above shows a vastly simplified example of the Swiss Cheese Model within the context of personal driving.

This multi-layered causal chain is represented by successive layers of Swiss cheese. While the cheese itself represents barriers to accident causation (labeled "Cheese" in the figure), holes in the cheese represent holes in those barriers; in other words, opportunities to complete the chain to an accident. On a good day, the path to an accident will be blocked by one or more layers of cheese. But, if the Swiss cheese holes line up for just a moment, the path to an accident is complete.

Referring to the figure, on a typical day, "safe road or traffic conditions" represents a barrier to an accident—a slice of Swiss cheese. On the other hand, hazardous conditions represent holes in that Swiss cheese slice—a failure of the first line of defense against an accident. But that may not be a problem for you if you remain alert (represented by the next layer of Swiss cheese). On another day, you may be overly fatigued, as indicated by holes in that second slice of Swiss cheese—or the second line of defense. This could be problematic except for the fact that you are aware that you are fatigued, and maintain a high level of situational awareness and avoid distraction (third layer). But let's say you drive in those hazardous conditions, while fatigued, and decide to engage in a cell phone conversation (negating the last line of defense). You may assume that, unlike with texting, since you can at least see the road while talking on a cell phone, there is no problem with doing so. But as we will discuss later, talking on a cell phone is a form of cognitive distraction that could complete the accident causal chain, even though you are looking where you are going. In the example in the figure, the holes line up and you have just caused an accident. It's your job to assess your behavioral traits, your physical condition and

24

your actions on the road, make an honest assessment of the layers of Swiss cheese in your specific driving situation, and, on any given day, prevent the "holes in the Swiss cheese from lining up."

Risk Management: One could say that safety is paramount in any activity and therefore no risks will be taken. However, this is an unrealistic premise. In aviation for instance, risks are real. They will never go away. Risks must be taken any time you engage in any truly worthwhile activity (except reading a book perhaps; and even then, you could get a paper cut which could become infected and…well never mind that). To drive a car, fly an airplane, fly in an airplane, to water ski or just walk across a road all entail risks. You must always assess whether the rewards are worth the risks. Driving for most of us, or at least being a passenger in a vehicle, is necessary for our very well-being. However, every reasonable precaution must be made while driving to avoid an accident. Can you accept taking the life of a loved one, a friend or someone else because of a brief act of carelessness? Abiding by the law, maintaining high situational awareness, making smart timely decisions based on that SA, and maneuvering safely all go a long way towards avoiding an injury or fatality on the road. The probability and severity of various risks associated with driving must be kept to a minimum. You owe that to you, your passengers, and other drivers, bicyclists, and pedestrians who share the transportation network with you. Before you drive, and while you drive, always assess yourself, your vehicle, and your environment—**Self, Vehicle, Environment**—to include traffic, road conditions and weather. If your risk factors are too high (you are too fatigued, stressed out, in too bad of a mood, too susceptible to distraction), then back off and change your physical or mental state; or don't drive.

Guidance in the remainder of this book will help you do this. Always consider the synergistic effect of the status, positive or negative, of specific factors in your driving domain—you, your vehicle, your environment. Know when to back off, to simplify, to change your attitude, put your phone away, drive slower, call for a ride.

We've already discussed how hazardous road conditions, fatigue and distraction can add up to cause an accident. But your own propensity for engaging in distracting activities may be all you need to cause, or become, a fatality. As another example, on a dry weather day, tires with low tread may be uneventful. But add in rainy weather, and you have an accident in the making.

Your Responsibility as a Driver: You take on a huge responsibility when driving. When you drive distracted, impaired or in a reckless manner, you are essentially using your vehicle as a lethal weapon. Perhaps if automobiles were registered weapons with associated legal accountability, then the importance of placing top priority on the task of driving—when driving—would be a "no-brainer."

A relatively small 3000-pound vehicle moving at 60 mph has 1000 times the energy of a bullet from a .357 Magnum handgun (a bullet is so deadly, of course, because its energy is concentrated in a very small area). A vehicle twice the mass of another vehicle has, perhaps intuitively, twice as much momentum and kinetic energy at a given speed as the vehicle half its mass (kinetic energy is the energy that any physical body has because it is in motion). Although changes in a vehicle's mass impart a linear change in kinetic energy (twice the mass, twice the kinetic energy), changes in a vehicle's velocity (speed) impart an exponential change in kinetic energy. For example, a vehicle traveling at twice the speed of another vehicle (of the same mass) has four times the kinetic energy of that slower vehicle. In a more practical example, a vehicle traveling at 75 mph, 40% faster than another vehicle traveling 55 mph, has approximately twice the kinetic energy as the slower one. Consider the effect of that additional energy in a head-on collision. If that is not daunting enough, an off-center collision presents its own hazards. Automobiles are designed to maximize collision safety during head-on collisions. In an off-center collision, your vehicle contacts an obstacle (another vehicle, or an immovable object such as a pole or tree) more towards the left or right front side. When this happens, your vehicle begins to rotate upon collision subjecting you and other occupants to torsional stresses that can damage the spine and move you away from front airbag protection. Off-center collisions can be deadly at collision speeds as low as 20-40 mph even though you are buckled in.

If we perceived ourselves driving a loaded weapon, we might naturally be more responsible when driving. And it may seem natural that we place higher priority on driving than on talking on a cell phone, but this is often simply not the case. When we drive in familiar conditions every day, we often subconsciously place very little priority on driving because the perceived threat to our life is low. We simply do not think that we could be seconds away from a life-threatening crisis. Staying between the lines on the road and staying a safe distance behind the car in front of us seems elementary.

Unless you are a beginner driver, it is easy to feel that you are the master of the road. Unfortunately, completely unanticipated driving hazards can rear their ugly heads in a split second; a vehicle swerving into your lane or jumping the median, someone slamming on the brakes in front of you, or perhaps a heavy chunk of rubber, metal bar or two-by-four a second away from slamming through your windshield. Because of missed cues or delayed reaction time due to not prioritizing tasks and allocating your attention correctly, the opportunity to respond in time may be missed, placing the lives of you the driver, and your passengers, or someone else outside the vehicle, in danger.

It is amazing how often people engage in activities other than driving, while driving; activities that can be very dangerous when you are the operator of a vehicle. The driver's job is driving, not talking, tending to children, etc. Distraction and inattention are very dangerous behaviors. And multitasking can be very dangerous, especially if priority of tasks is on something other than driving. A driver oftentimes has very little response time before another vehicle or an obstacle on the edge of the road becomes a lethal hazard. Even a fighter pilot flying low and fast, say, 500 mph and 500 feet above the ground, may have more time to respond to a flight path deviation resulting from distraction than a driver has time to respond to a lane deviation or other hazard due to distraction from the task of driving. A fighter pilot in a steep banked high-G turn may inadvertently overbank, increasing the aircraft's bank angle say from 75 degrees from wings level to 90 degrees of bank while "checking 6" or looking behind his or her aircraft to check for surface or airborne threats. Doing so would cause the aircraft to accelerate towards the ground; yet the pilot would still have two to three seconds to detect and react to the overbank to avoid ground impact. This is still more time than a driver might have to avoid a collision after a very short period of distraction, given that road vehicles operate so close to other vehicles and obstacles.

Gaining and maintaining high SA is a discipline and an art. A two to three second reaction time may not sound like much time. Consider that, on the roadway, where potentially lethal obstacles are oftentimes just feet away, a vehicle driver who becomes distracted for even a second or two may be unable to avoid a serious accident. You can even be "in the right" and still be involved in a serious accident that you could have avoided simply by being more attentive and by driving defensively. You can drive without incident 999 times (less than a year's worth of driving for someone that uses their vehicle for transportation to and from work and for getting around in general). But can you afford to become a statistic on that thousandth drive, or cause a loved one or someone else to become a statistic? It is easy to become complacent when driving seems routine. But the driving environment has a habit of throwing an unanticipated curveball at the least opportune time. You may think you have high SA when driving. But maybe you are just lucky and someday fate will catch up. Do not let that happen. Take matters into your own hand. Learn to drive without distraction and with high situational awareness all the time.

CHAPTER THREE: DISTRACTION — THE NEMESIS OF SA

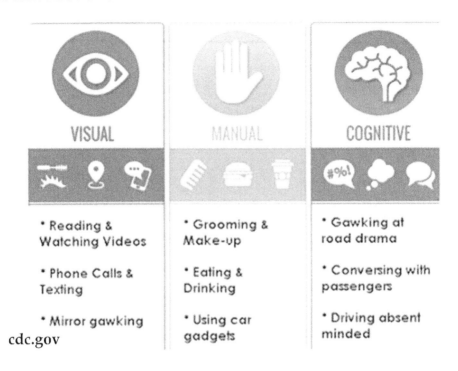

VISUAL	MANUAL	COGNITIVE
• Reading & Watching Videos	• Grooming & Make-up	• Gawking at road drama
• Phone Calls & Texting	• Eating & Drinking	• Conversing with passengers
• Mirror gawking	• Using car gadgets	• Driving absent minded

cdc.gov

Types of Distraction: Because the driving environment is very dynamic and changes rapidly over time, maintaining high SA, as we shall see, involves continuous active scanning and avoidance of distraction. Distraction is the nemesis of situational awareness. You might ask how a momentary distraction could significantly affect your level of SA. The reason for this is because your SA while moving at 55 mph on a road is extremely fleeting. At this speed, you are traveling a football field's length in a little under four seconds. Two vehicles approaching each other on a two-lane road at 55 mph are closing that same football field's length in under two seconds. You can lose enough SA in a second or two to be at extremely high risk of an accident, if for instance, your vehicle or someone else's strays from its lane. And even if distractions are very short, frequent short distractions can erode SA or keep it at dangerously low levels.

I was on my way to the local Air Force Base in Arizona to fly one day, when I witnessed a large black pick-up truck directly in front of me plow into the back of a sedan that had slowed in rush hour traffic. The visibility was excellent and the road was dry. I pulled up behind the pick-up to check on both drivers, who were OK. The young male driver in the pick-up, who was on his way to work, was obviously shaken up. He looked at me somewhat confused and said he had just picked up his soda drink to take a sip, and the next thing he knew, he hit the car in front of him. This was a classic case of distraction and shows how quickly conditions can become prime for an accident, especially in dynamic or rapidly changing conditions. It takes time to build up SA. And then you must maintain it. There are three main forms of distraction when driving; **visual, cognitive**, and **manual (physical)** distraction (see the above figure).

Visual Distraction: Driving is an extremely visually oriented task. Until widely fielded technology affords otherwise, there is no way around that. Visual distraction, or taking your eyes off the task of driving, can be deadly. Your human brain, while in motion, is a very poor determiner of where you are and where you are going when you are visually distracted, especially when you are moving at road or highway speeds. Your brain can lie to you very quickly about where you are on the road surface when your visual attention is directed elsewhere. Your vestibular system, which provides a sense of motion, balance and spatial orientation, and your temporal awareness—your awareness of the passage of time—do not work very well when you are distracted. It is very difficult for anyone to keep their place on the road surface, and to mentally keep track of other vehicles and obstacles when looking somewhere other than the road ahead. It is also impossible to react to a developing bad situation when you are not looking at the road.

As dangerous as it is to look away from the road, it is much more dangerous to turn and look behind you while driving—at least if not performed correctly. Of course, you should physically turn and look rearward occasionally to clear your vehicle's blind spots, since there is always the possibility of missing another vehicle (especially a smaller vehicle such as a motorcycle), if you rely solely on your side and rearview mirrors to clear behind you. But if you look rearward in an exaggerated way, several potentially problematic physiological events occur. First, you remove your vision, peripheral and central, completely from the road ahead. Second, when rotating your head, you introduce a motion input into your vestibular system which can be disorienting and may cause you to make an erroneous input in steering. Third, if you rotate your torso while looking back, any inadvertent arm motion may also cause you to introduce an unintended movement on the steering wheel. For these reasons, it is inadvisable to reach into the back seat to tend to children or to grab something off the seat, unless you can keep your eyes on the road ahead. If there is an emergency, and you must look and reach back, then pull over first.

Although you will have to look back to each side periodically to check your blind spots, keeping your SA high and setting up your seat and mirrors properly can minimize time spent doing so. When you do look back, move your head while minimizing upper torso movement. Use some of your peripheral vision to see rearward, keeping some peripheral vision aimed forward. And only look back very briefly. The human vestibular system has not yet evolved to the level where we can sense our location and position in space when not looking where we are going. If only we were birds…

Cognitive (Mental) Distraction: Cognitive distraction in the driving domain occurs when you are perhaps looking at the road ahead, but you are devoting your mental attention to a non-driving task such as talking on a cell phone, sending a voice text message, or listening to directions on your phone or from your GPS personal assistant. You may perceive some of the visual information about the road conditions and traffic ahead, but you may not process that information effectively. Of course, this applies to the other senses (you "hear" something but do not process the information). That's right. You can physically be looking at something and not be comprehending what you are looking at. And even though you perceive certain visual cues when cognitively distracted, you still miss important details in the scene.

Have you ever been preoccupied while driving, so much so that, as you became aware again of where you were, you wondered how you got there or how you even stayed on the road? Perhaps you were daydreaming, stressed out about work, or preoccupied in some other similar cognitive distraction. Your eyes were "aimed" at the road ahead, but they were not focusing on anything. Zoning out in this case, for whatever reason, can shut down your brain. You may perceive information about the environment ahead of you. But 90% of it may be useless information if your brain does not process it or if you cannot make any decisions, proactive or reactive, based on that information. Your brain may only be processing enough driving related information to keep you within the lane markers. What would then happen if someone swerved or crossed the median in front of you, or if a large piece of road debris penetrated your windshield while you were "zoning out?" General anxiety or stress and fatigue can have similar effects on your visual perception and comprehension.

Manual (or Physical) Distraction: Manual distraction occurs when you remove your hands from the steering wheel, for instance, to pick up something like food, a drink or a cell phone. Have you ever driven with your knees, freeing your hands to perform a secondary task? If it became necessary for you to maneuver to avoid something at that moment, you would not be able to do it safely.

While on the topic of keeping your hands on the steering wheel, many driving experts now recommend placing your hands at the 9 and 3 o'clock position or even the 8 and 4 positions on the steering wheel versus the traditional 10 and 2 positions (the 8 and 4 o'clock position does not provide as much maneuvering leverage as the 9 and 3 position). Doing so lessens risk of unnecessary injury if the driver side airbag in the steering wheel deploys, while still affording good maneuvering potential. You must do your own research to determine where it is safest to have your hands on the steering wheel based on your own vehicle manufacturer's recommendations and your comfort level. Regardless, having two hands on the steering wheel is the best bet if you must maneuver aggressively. If you think about it, having only one hand on the steering will not serve you well if you are forced to maneuver suddenly. Also, the steering wheel could be jerked out of your hand by a mechanical failure with your tire, wheel or steering. One word of caution. When you steer, try not to cross your arms (which can occur with "hand-over-hand" steering) if there is the slightest chance you will hit something. Doing so can result in added injury if the steering column airbag deploys while your arms crossed. It may be best to use the push-pull-slide ("hand-to-hand") method of steering, when practical, given possible deployment of the airbag in a collision (you can check out some videos on this technique on YouTube).

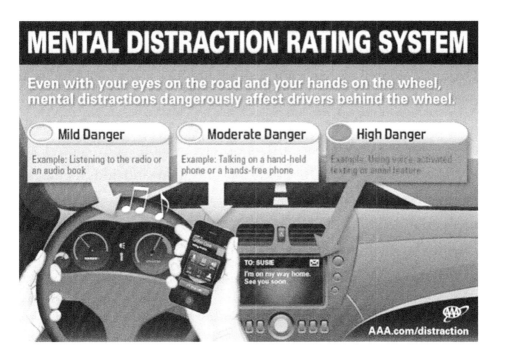

The Cost of Distraction: The figure above shows the dangers of distraction. Regardless of the cause, distraction has these negative effects. Your visual scanning is hampered; the speed and accuracy with which you can identify roadway objects and hazards is impaired; your ability to make potentially life-saving decisions is adversely impacted; your reaction time is slowed. When you text and drive, you are unfortunately engaged in all three forms of distraction; visual, cognitive and manual. You are a driving menace. Can you live with the potential consequences? Sending a voice text with hands-free technology is still dangerous because of the higher level of cognitive distraction. Even when you use technology that allows you to keep your eyes on the road, the cognitive distraction of tending to any mental task other than driving can cause you to miss enough visual cues to have an accident.

The Dangerous Effects of Alcohol and Similar Substances When Driving: Alcohol affects your driving abilities in the same ways as distraction. However, unlike texting, where you are immediately and absolutely distracted, alcohol is more insidious, at least to the driver under the influence. Alcohol impairs both your central and peripheral vision, lessens your concentration and judgment, and hampers coordination. It slows reaction time. Worse, it makes you more confident at a time when your driving skills are significantly impaired. Other substances, including some legal prescription and over-the-counter drugs can have similar debilitating effects on driving.

CHAPTER FOUR: SA DEFINED

© Karl Schlimm

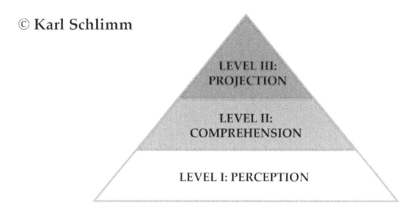

There are many different definitions of situational awareness, or SA, to suit different needs. One of the most prevalent definitions of SA, especially in the aviation community, comes from Dr. Mica Endsley, PhD, and former President and CEO of SA Technologies. SA Technologies specializes in the development of operator interfaces and associated situational awareness enhancement not only in the aviation industry, but also the medical field, oil and gas industry, air traffic control, and the U.S. Military. As you can see, situational awareness has far reaching applications. Dr. Endsley's definition of SA is as follows:

"Situational awareness is the perception of the elements within the environment within a volume of time and space, the comprehension of their meaning and the projection of their status into the future."

I'll expand on this definition in my own words for clarity:

"Situational awareness is the perception of elements (vehicles, obstacles, road surface, weather, etc.) in your environment using your senses (vision, hearing, touch, smell), comprehending them to form a mental model or "visualization" of your environment tailored to your goals or priorities, and then predicting their future state to make effective decisions. It is enhanced by knowledge, experience, training and practice."

At the risk of oversimplifying things, SA is the state of knowing what is going on around you.

What's up

Levels of SA: Perception of elements within your environment using all your senses (vision, hearing, touch, smell) is **Level 1 SA**. This is only the first, most basic level. It does you little good if you do not take it any further, for instance, because you are fatigued or busily engaged in conversation while driving. And if you miss the opportunity to perceive environmental cues vital to your well-being, then you have not even reached level 1 SA.

significance

Level 2 SA is the comprehension of the significance of elements that you perceive in your environment. For instance, if you perceive a vehicle in your left rear-view mirror that is getting larger (level 1 SA), then you comprehend that it is "closing," or getting closer to you (level 2 SA).

future

Level 3 SA is the highest level of SA, and this is the ability to project the status or significance of elements within your environment (vehicles, road obstacles, traffic control and signage, etc.) into the future. Predicting the future state of environmental elements is essential to making effective decisions. As an example, your level 3 SA of that closing vehicle on your left tells you that it will pass you in approximately 20 seconds, and that if you want to move into the lane to your left, you should do it now while not being a safety concern to the approaching vehicle. Otherwise, you must wait to change lanes until it passes.

SA Priorities: You cannot maintain situational awareness on all elements in your driving or operating domain. You must pay attention to the appropriate few elements in any given situation that will maximize your ability to drive safely.

You could have very high level 3 SA on some elements in your environment, but perhaps no SA on other elements because of poor visual scanning or not prioritizing elements to pay attention to effectively. As an example, you may have level 3 SA on vehicles ahead of you but you may have completely overlooked the construction ladder lying on the road surface in your lane immediately ahead. As another example, you might have high awareness of other elements in your driving domain but low awareness of the maintenance status of your vehicle, which could cause you to have an accident if a critical component of your vehicle fails due to neglect. Perhaps you may drive in a foreign country where you could be very attentive to the driving environment but unable to make consistently good decisions because you lack knowledge of local driving laws, customs, road signage, etc. In this example, even though you may exercise extreme diligence in visual scanning and maintaining high SA, your poor knowledge base of foreign laws limits your level 3 SA and decision-making ability. By the way, this is why you are so comfortable (and complacent) in familiar driving conditions. Have you ever noticed that even driving in unfamiliar conditions in your own state or country can significantly add to your stress level and driving work load?

You cannot possibly have high SA on every element in your driving domain. Generally, having level 3 SA presumes you have that level of SA on all those elements that are most critical to your immediate and near-term safety and well-being, and then preferably, but not critically, those elements that are important to your other driving priorities, such as navigation. Focused scanning and attention to sensory cues based on what you are doing or want to do when driving is very important.

In driving, to build SA, you must have your objectives or priorities straight. Your number one priority should always be to keep you and your passengers safe and alive while not injuring or killing anyone else on the road. Any other priority, whether it be getting from point A to point B, finding a place to get fuel or food, sightseeing, checking on children, or reaching for something in the back seat, takes "second seat." This may seem obvious to you, but how many times have you seen a driver illegally veer across an off-ramp gore (the triangular road section between solid white lines before an exit or onramp) kicking up debris just to make an exit when it would have cost just an extra few minutes to continue to the next exit and backtrack? Anyone in that impulsive a mindset probably has low SA of vehicles and other hazards in the vicinity and is taking an unacceptable risk.

Even if that driver had enough SA to know he or she would not hit anyone, impulsive driving behavior is dangerous and can significantly increase the potential for a collision or vehicle loss of control. You may be impulsive by nature, but having the mindset that safety is always number one priority even if it causes inconvenience will help you prevent an accident.

Your Mental Model: A mental model (also called a cognitive map, frame of reference, or the "mind's eye") is a mental or cognitive representation of the real world, or certain aspects of it. To create your mental model of what is happening around you, and how it is changing over time, you must scan visually, paying attention to those elements in the environment most important to your safety, and then to your other priorities.

Objective-Oriented Visual Scanning: What you pay most attention to while driving depends on your objectives. As discussed, safety always comes first. Only after that can you focus on other tasks such as navigating from point A to point B.

A far from all-inclusive list of elements in the driving environment or domain that you should pay attention to are the following: Your location on the road surface, and your location relative to other traffic and obstacles; weather and road conditions; objects or debris on the road surface ahead; road curvature; road signage and alerts; traffic control changes ahead; location of traffic ahead, to the sides, and behind you; distance, and relative speed of vehicles in your vicinity; other driver behavior; pedestrians; where to go and how to get there if you have an immediate problem; your current navigation status; and vehicle systems and fuel indications and status.

Hypnoart/Pixabay

This objective-oriented visual scanning allows you to create a mental representation or visualization—a "mental model"—of your environment that is as accurate as possible with respect to the real world around you, and to keep it accurate as your environment changes in time. Of course, a wealth of data from your other senses (hearing, tactile sense or touch, perhaps even smell) is fed into your mental model to make it more complete and meaningful, so do not discount the importance of those other senses to detect changes in your environment, including your vehicle.

There are also the non-sensory factors that form a more complete mental model. As previously mentioned, your overall driving experience as factors in significantly to your ability to engage in high SA and decision making. Also important is your knowledge of pre-existing conditions such as your overall health, not to mention your current level of alertness; your driving experience and limitations; the maintenance status or health of your vehicle, etc.

You must also consider various sources of potential distractions—phone, passengers, GPS, radio, etc.—and have an unceasing conscious mental discipline to keep those distractions to a minimum.

Your Mental Model is Not a Complete Picture of the Real World:
There is, in almost all situations, way too much information in your local environment for you to perceive, much less for your brain to process. To complicate matters, having expectations of what your environment should be like, based on what you have seen in the past, may cause you to miss certain elements in your environment that pose a hazard to you, because they lie outside of your expectations. This is a form of confirmation bias, and it can get you into trouble. As an example, if you have an expectation that all drivers will have their headlights on at dusk or dawn, you may not consciously detect an unlighted vehicle approaching in the lane you are about to turn into, when driving under those dimly lit conditions. In this example, since you are only consciously scanning for headlights, and not vehicles, you may only see the closest lighted vehicle which happens to be a safe distance away; and you may miss the unlighted vehicle you are about to turn into, presenting a collision hazard. This is more of a probable occurrence than you

might think for two reasons. First, drivers forget to turn on their headlights all the time or feel that it is unnecessary to turn lights on at dusk or dawn; and second, bright lights constrict your pupils making it more difficult to see dim and low contrast objects under those conditions. It does not matter if the driver of that unlit vehicle made a poor decision if a collision occurs.

Kaspars Eberlins

You make decisions based on your mental model—your perception of the real world. Again, this is not a complete model of the real world. There are probably many elements missing, like a puzzle with pieces missing. Fortunately, you only need a mental model of your surroundings sufficient to support your objectives and to keep you safe. You can get a reasonably accurate picture of a thousand-piece puzzle with half of the puzzle pieces missing—if you see the right puzzle pieces—even though much detail is absent. The human brain is good at filling in missing details to form a coherent picture.

Regarding an incomplete mental model, if you drive at a constant speed in the right lane, it may not matter that you do not see the car in your blind spot, assuming you do not encounter a situation necessitating maneuvering into that lane. In fact, if you do not perceive it as being there, then that car is missing completely in your mental model of your surroundings. If you decide to change lanes far enough in advance of when you feel you need to, then you can "sample" or scan your environment at your leisure...and build SA to a level sufficient to support your decision and action to change lanes. In this case, you have time to scan and detect or perceive the presence of that car in your blind spot.

The Importance of Having SA Before You Need It: If you must react suddenly however, then optimally you would have already built up a preexisting level of high SA which includes the awareness of that vehicle. The fact that there may be vehicles very near you or converging with you that are "out of sight, out of mind" can be a very dangerous situation if you must maneuver defensively in a crisis, so it is best to maintain high SA even when you do not think you need it. Although your mental model is never complete with respect to the real world, it must be complete enough to allow you to make safe driving decisions.

Much has been written on defensive driving and on making good driving decisions. A driver must have high situational awareness to reliably and consistently make effective decisions. Fortunately, the art of gaining and maintaining high SA can be practiced and perfected. High SA is fleeting, however. When driving, tasks such as thorough and effective visual scanning to maintain this level of SA must continuously be performed. Not only can a simple breakdown in maintaining SA, such as not looking both ways when crossing an intersection, cause an accident, but being unprepared for unpredictable driving hazards can also be deadly. Driving seems so easy yet accidents still frequently occur to people like you and me who thought they were aware while driving. When you can plan a driving task in advance, you often have time to look around, gather information, and evaluate alternative actions. There is, in this case, time to build SA to suit your objectives or priorities. If you decide to get fuel in the next twenty miles or so, you have time to search for nearest gas stations while minimizing distraction, evaluate which one is best, and then clear your path to the exit.

Again, when driving, you must always be prepared to react quickly in a crisis, perhaps to stop suddenly or to maneuver quickly to avoid road debris or a collision with another vehicle. Maneuvering aggressively may be required but can only be done safely if you do not over control—a common error—and you already know the location of other vehicles and obstacles around you before you maneuver, including vehicles in your blind spots. This means your SA must be high before the crisis occurs, because there is no time to gain required SA when you have a split second to react. Keeping your SA elevated when you don't need it is important so that you have high SA when you do need it in a hurry.

Here is another example of the importance of having high situational awareness before you need it. Let's say you are driving on a busy highway at rush hour. The roads are wet and traffic is heavy. You notice that the left shoulder is very narrow against the highway divider. You are in the left middle lane and have been scanning frequently for traffic all around you. You know there is a truck on your left, a car behind you in your lane, and no one in the next lane to your right alongside or behind you for about three car lengths. Suddenly your engine quits. You are faced with either stopping on a busy highway with aggressive fast-moving traffic in wet conditions or, alternatively, with efficiently maneuvering to the side of the road; but which side? Since you already have a mental image of traffic in your vicinity, as well as road and shoulder conditions, you determine in a split second that you can—and probably should— begin maneuvering to the right. You therefore maneuver deftly into the next lane to the right while clearing for traffic in the right-most lane. As you see a truck going by you in that lane, you are now clear to pull off to the side of the road. In this case, having high SA before you needed it allowed you avoid startle or panic, and to make a smart and immediate decision to maneuver to the better side of the road under current conditions without hitting anyone. By having high SA, you avoided becoming stranded at a stop in the middle of a busy road.

Would you have reacted safely if you were zoning out or distracted, for instance, by a cell phone call? What if a vehicle was about to pass you on your right, but you did not see it, and so you maneuvered to the right under the false assumption that no vehicle was there, only to hit that vehicle in the lane to your right? Clearly critical split-second decisions require that you have an accurate mental representation of the real world around you. To have that, you must proactively and continuously keep your level of SA high. Focusing on the task of driving, while driving, may save your life someday.

Not knowing in advance what is going on around you can prove costly. The level of your SA may mean the difference between life and death on the road. So many hazards exist, many of which remain hidden most of the time. Practicing high SA makes you better at achieving high SA. Conversely, if you make a habit of being distracted, you will never learn how to achieve high SA and must rely on the odds being in your favor to avoid an accident. Even a driver with years of experience driving, who makes a continuous habit of being distracted on the phone or texting while driving, being overly fatigued or zoning out or all the above, will never become a good driver. High SA will keep you from being surprised and being reactive, and will enable you to proactively make time-critical lifesaving decisions. Achieving and maintaining a high level of situational awareness takes knowledge, training and practice.

The Role of Experience in Driving: As much as any sufficiently distracted driver is a threat on the road, an inexperienced driver who allows him- or herself to become distracted is a ticking time bomb. Experience plays a large role in having high SA, but only if you are a habitually focused driver. Of course, an alert, conscientious, albeit inexperienced driver is probably safer than any experienced driver who is distracted.

The following example might shed some light on how easy it is for us to take our experience in any complex activity like driving for granted. Let's say you were to invite someone who has lived in a tiny remote mountain village in a remote part of the world to drive with you; someone who has never seen any mode of transportation other than by foot and perhaps a mule. While driving with you, he may perceive the road, traffic, signs, and other items of interest in the driving environment, but have absolutely no idea of their significance. He could certainly engage in level 1 SA—perception, to a limited extent, as he takes in all the fantastic and new, if not overwhelming sensory cues. However, he would have limited or no ability to engage in level 2 SA—comprehension of what these sensory cues mean. After all, he has never seen automobiles, paved roads, signs, etc. Therefore, he could not possibly achieve level 3 SA—predicting future states to be able to make effective decisions.

Similarly, it is more difficult for a young inexperienced driver to gain and maintain high SA on the road than it is for an experienced driver. There are so many elements of the driving domain that the inexperienced driver has not seen, and so many decision-making scenarios that he or she has not yet experienced. Of course, by the time the average young driver gets a driver's permit, he or she has already most likely spent years as a passenger in a vehicle and understands many aspects of the driving domain. But comprehending or having level 2 SA on many of the elements of the driving environment is just a start. The new driver must now actually drive a vehicle in myriad traffic conditions, learn to scan all the elements of the environment most critical to his or her safety and make important decisions, learn to assess relative speed and closure, and predict how these very dynamic driving elements will come together at some point in the future – not an easy task. However, inexperienced drivers can quickly achieve a decent level of skill and confidence on the road by being attentive. Always be aware and ready, though. Just as you feel that you are the expert in predicting what those drivers around you will do, one of them could, at any time, do something you could not have predicted.

The Myth of Multitasking: Most of us take pride in what we call multitasking, or performing two or more tasks at the same time. Regardless of how multitasking is defined, the brain cannot normally perform two or more complex or high-level cognitive tasks simultaneously. Driving and talking on a cell phone are considered complex cognitive tasks. The brain can, however, rapidly sequence or time-share attention between tasks. However, your brain's potential, as good as it is, and your actual abilities at any given time, may be two different things all together.

Here is the inherent problem. Engaging in more than one complex cognitive task affords your brain less time to devote to any single task. Moreover, as the complexity and perceived priority of one task increases, the mental processing time typically devoted to the other complex task diminishes. If the task that you give less priority to is the task of driving, you are opening yourself up to missing critical sensory cues such as seeing the brake lights - or misjudging the distance - of the car in front of you.

You naturally devote more time to the task that you place the most priority on. If you must talk on a cell phone in traffic, even using hands-free technology, it is imperative that you place much less priority on that task than on driving (remember it is illegal in some

kubko/123RF

states and countries to physically hold a cell phone or even for young drivers to make any kind of phone call while driving, hands-free or otherwise). Always make driving a priority. Remember, just because you are using hands free technology or are looking at the road ahead does not mean you will be able to keep your SA high while multitasking. When you multitask, your visual scan and mental processing devoted to driving diminish.

CHAPTER FIVE: A MODEL OF DRIVER SA

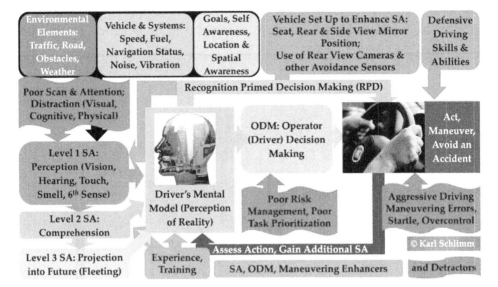

A Model of Driver Situational Awareness

L et's build a simple model of driver situational awareness, that you can use to guide you as you build your SA expertise. As you read through this guide, please reference the above figure depicting my model of driver SA frequently (if the image is in black and white in your print version of this book, then there will be a detailed color version of the image on the front cover). Hopefully it will make better sense as you complete your study of the concepts contained in it.

Please notice in the figure above, the many elements of the driving domain that we have discussed, or will discuss, the levels of SA, and elements of decision-making. Also, note in light blue, some enhancers of SA; and in red, some of the detractors of SA. Again, this figure will make more sense once you have read this guide

---

completely. I will suggest that the primary areas of SA that you must pay attention to when driving are in the following categories to be discussed in this chapter: Goal awareness, self-awareness, vehicle and systems awareness, critical action procedures, maneuvering awareness, wingman awareness, navigation awareness, spatial awareness, environmental awareness, threat awareness, and temporal awareness. Your list may vary depending on your driving environment.

Goals, Self Awareness, Location & Spatial Awareness

Goal Awareness: Your objectives while driving determine, to an extent, what elements of your environment you pay most attention to. You should always build a dynamic awareness, tailored to your goals or objectives, of the location of other vehicles, obstacles and hazards around you, as well as vehicle trends. Although you scan and build SA mainly to suit your primary objectives, you should always devote some of your SA maintenance towards planning for potential problems or contingencies. This can be called a "What-If" analysis (in flying, it is part of Threat and Error Management). For instance, you could ask yourself periodically, "What if my tire fails now," or "What if the car ahead slams on its brakes," etc. You cannot do this effectively if you are distracted! You should always know where you can maneuver if you must, to avoid something, or if you have a problem. The time to determine if someone is immediately behind you and to your right, for instance, is not when you have an urgent situation necessitating maneuvering into the right lane. And if you make a habit of being distracted and not directing attention to building SA, you are setting yourself up for failure.

Always place safety ahead of other objectives. For instance, if you must turn left into heavy traffic, and then plan to move right two or three lanes to reach an on-ramp close by, it is wise to not ever get into the mindset that you must do whatever it takes to reach that on-ramp. There will be times where you miss your navigation goal because of traffic. Barreling across three lanes, or slowing in your lane immediately after merging in front of heavy traffic, is not the right answer. In other words, do not let your "mission" goal of getting somewhere negate your safety goal of not having an accident. safety > goals

Having the mindset of getting what you want no matter what the potential risks will set you up for disaster. Sometimes you will be inconvenienced. If you remind yourself often that smooth, safe, predictable and compassionate driving is always paramount, you may just prevent yourself from becoming a maneuvering statistic, which could happen if, for instance, if you make a desperate impulsive attempt to make an exit you did not notice until the last second. Aviation history is filled with accident reports and fatalities because pilots were intent on getting to their destination regardless of deteriorating weather, low fuel conditions, fatigue, etc. Your

#1 Goal: safety
#2 Goal - Getting there

number one goal when driving is to survive and let others survive regardless of whether you get to your destination on time or at all. You will miss the exit sometimes. You will be late for work sometimes. If you always accept that, you will be a safer driver.

Self-Awareness: This is an awareness of your personal driving level of experience both in general, and within the context of your current driving environment. It is also an awareness of your physical and mental state, your behavioral predisposition due to your dominant attitudes, and your associated limitations because of your behavioral disposition.

Your Experience: Regarding your experience as a driver, consider your overall experience. But also, take a hard look at your experience driving in your current driving environment. You may have spent most of your driving time going to and from work in familiar conditions. But how experienced are you in an environment such as the following: at night, in the wintertime, on unfamiliar desolate roads, in blowing snow and wondering why there is a car spun out in the median every half-mile? I experienced this driving environment recently while traveling through New Mexico, and I can tell you that I would have rather been in a jet fighter on final approach to land at night going 180 mph, then in those conditions. Something told me then and there that I should NOT be driving. Sometimes it is best to pull off the road, and, in this case, to find a motel for the night.

Your Physical State: Also, consider your physical state. Are you well rested or tired? Are you feeling well or feeling ill? Consider this: there are probably an astounding number of fatigued drivers on the road. At least one vehicle near you on the road at any given time probably contains a fatigued driver. Lack of sleep is a worldwide epidemic of sorts. Have you ever performed an "unintentional lane change" due to fatigue?

Look back at the driving fatality statistics. The primary cause of a full one third of driving fatalities in the before-mentioned statistical summary was due to failure of the driver to remain in his or her lane or on the road surface. Using your intuition, would it not be reasonable to assume that many these fatalities were due, aside from distraction, to the driver being overly fatigued or falling asleep at the wheel?

Unfortunately, the manifestations of fatigue can creep up on a driver very insidiously. Your first clue that you are tired may just be that unintentional lane change. This is your final warning. Ideally you would not have gotten behind the wheel in this condition in the first place. You may not be so lucky next time. Your goal now becomes immediately finding a place to pull over safely. Get out, stretch out, do some push-ups, eat or drink something that can give you an energy boost. Do not get behind the wheel if there is any risk of falling asleep. You can be charged for vehicular homicide if you kill someone because you fell asleep at the wheel—especially if the court can prove that you were negligent because you had no sleep, for instance, in the past 36 hours and still chose to drive.

Your Mental State: Considering your mental state: are you relaxed, anxious, or stressed out because of personal or professional issues? Perhaps you are predisposed to mental distraction. Many people are anxious and mentally preoccupied by nature. This is a limitation that you must work around while driving. Also, consider your behavioral predisposition due to your ingrained attitudes. Hazardous attitudes typically defined as the following in the aviation world are also applicable to driving:

Валерий Качаев/123RF

1. Anti-Authority (*"Don't Tell Me"*): You resent rules and regulations. You disregard the law because you do not like people telling you what to do, or perhaps you feel entitled to do so.

2. Impulsive (*"Do Something Quickly"*): You react impulsively, making last second decisions without considering the consequences—like veering across the exit gore because you almost missed your exit.

3. Invulnerability (*"It Won't Happen to Me"*): You feel accidents happen to other people. Those that have been involved in a serious accident probably felt the same way up until the accident.

4. Macho (*"I Can Do It"*): You try to prove you are better than everyone else. Of course, this is not just a male trait.

5. Resignation (*"What's the Use"*): You feel that anything you do will not make much difference in what happens to you. Perhaps you habitually avoid wearing your seat belt. If things go well, luck is on your side. If things do not go well, then someone is out to get you, or it was just your time.

Road Rage: In the driving environment, road rage is a common behavior that can be the result of a variety of hazardous attitudes. Ava Cadell, PhD, a psychologist and instructor at the Institute for the Advanced Study of Human Sexuality in San Francisco, stated the following: "The heavy metal of a car is a safe-haven. Road "ragers" don't think about the consequences or even about other people on the road as real people with real families…road ragers are selfish, power hungry, angry, and vindictive."

In a July 2016 article posted on the web site of The American Automobile Association (AAA), Tamra Johnson, Manager, AAA Public Relations, stated that a recent study released by the AAA Foundation for Traffic Safety found that nearly 80 percent of drivers expressed significant anger, aggression or road rage behind the wheel at least once in the past year. More incredible is that approximately eight million U.S. drivers have engaged in extreme examples of road rage, including using firearms, purposefully ramming another vehicle, or getting out of the car to confront another driver. From the point of view of situational awareness this is an important topic. You need to know that there are other drivers on the road that are a hazard to you; and you need to watch out for them, and how to potentially deal with them. Also, you need to know that you have the potential to be a serious threat to other drivers on the road if you engage in, or are prone to engaging in, these behaviors. The AAA study found that U.S. drivers surveyed, engaged in the following road rage behaviors:

1. Purposefully tailgating: 51 percent (104 million drivers)

2. Yelling at another driver: 47 percent (95 million drivers)

3. Honking to show annoyance or anger: 45 percent (91 million drivers)

4. Making angry gestures: 33 percent (67 million drivers)

5. Trying to block another vehicle from changing lanes: 24 percent (49 million drivers)

6. Cutting off another vehicle on purpose: 12 percent (24 million drivers)

7. Getting out of the vehicle to confront another driver: 4 percent (7.6 million drivers)

8. Bumping or ramming another vehicle on purpose: 3 percent (5.7 million drivers)

Of those eight road rage behaviors, the first and the last four are indicative of serious and dangerous attitude problems which, if seen, must be reported to authorities. If you have personally engaged in these activities, your behavioral disposition is a hazard to other drivers!

Are you well-balanced, or predisposed to anger and road rage? Do you automatically want to punish a driver who wrongs you or cuts in front of you? Then let's face it, you are a danger to other drivers and you need to keep your behavior in check. Alternatively, if you are predisposed to forgive other drivers when they inconvenience you—realizing that either they might be in a hurry or distressed for valid reasons, or perhaps you have done the same at times because you were in a rush—then you are setting yourself up for success. For your SA, to prevent road rage, follow these tips:

Never make someone as you.

1. Don't Offend: Never cause another driver to change their speed or direction. That means not forcing another driver to use their brakes, or turn their steering wheel in response to something you have done.

2. Be Tolerant and Forgiving: The other driver may just be having a bad day. Assume that the driver did not intend for you to take his or her actions personally. And even if it is obvious that the driver's actions were intentional, then you should take the moral high ground and show restraint. When you do that, you grow stronger in character. When you get down in the weeds with the other driver and duke it out, then you have just compromised your character, and have entered the mix of two out-of-control drivers who pose a risk to themselves and other people.

3. Do Not Respond: Avoid eye contact, don't make gestures, maintain space around your vehicle and contact 9-1-1 if needed.

Barry Markell, PhD, a psychotherapist, recommends that the victim of road rage take control of the situation since the road rage driver is most likely incapable in the moment of controlling his or her behavior. Markell specifically recommends the following:

1. If you are being tailgated, change lanes.
2. If someone wants to pass, slow down and let them.
3. Do not return gestures.
4. At all costs, stay behind drivers who are angry. They can do less damage if you are behind them.
5. If necessary, pull off the road or take an exit and let them go on by.
6. Do not make eye contact.

Dr. Cadell disagrees, however, with the recommendation not to make eye contact. She thinks it is important to look at the offending driver, not only to see them as a human being, but also to identify them later.

Vehicle & Systems: Speed, Fuel, Navigation Status, Noise, Vibration

Vehicle & Systems Awareness: This is an awareness of your automobile and its associated systems. Most of us take our vehicle for granted. But if we want to be safe drivers, our familiarity with our car, SUV or truck must go beyond how to adjust the mirrors, shift into drive, steer our way to work, and brake to a stop to park. And technology, at least as we typically think of technology, is not a save-all. A good driver in a basic no-frills car will always be safer than a bad driver in the most technologically advanced car, at least until technology can reliably remove the poor or distracted driver from the loop. Knowing your vehicle, whether it be an automobile, a boat, a fighter jet, Boeing 777, is a critical part of situational awareness. How well you know your vehicle in terms of performance capabilities and limitations, field of view limitations, safety features and status, and the health of mechanical components, can make the difference between avoiding a crash or being involved in one, and how well you survive that crash.

One with your Vehicle: Consider that you and your vehicle are "one"—an integrated human/machine system. You are one with your vehicle when you strap into it, set it up properly, feel comfortable with it, and can make it do what you want it to, within its limitations and yours, and within legal and responsible constraints, without risking an accident.

Any good pilot—a properly trained pilot—feels "one" with the airplane, no matter how large or complex it is. That pilot will then, as a seamless and integral part of the overall human-machine system, know how to right him- or herself, and hence the aircraft if it is somehow upset beyond acceptable airspeed, pitch and bank parameters; as if the aircraft and its flight controls are an extension of the human will and physiology. Just the same, a good driver knows his or her vehicle well enough to be able to be one with it. This means, for instance, that you, the driver, should not drive a vehicle too large or too complex for your capabilities, at least not until proper training is obtained; and then you should drive within your comfort zone as you gain experience and confidence.

Seat Belts: Before we get much further, the importance of being properly restrained in any moving vehicle cannot be overemphasized. A pilot would not even think about flying an aircraft without being properly restrained. Why would you drive a motor vehicle without buckling up? And why would you drive without all your passengers, including your children, being properly restrained? To not insist that you and your passengers be properly restrained, and remain so while your vehicle is in motion, is to be about as intelligent as an egg—an egg in a jar, waiting to be rattled around and shattered against the walls if the jar is shaken. If you drive without seat belts and shoulder harnesses (if available), or drive while allowing passengers to be similarly unrestrained, then you might want to seriously reevaluate your priorities. Driving unrestrained vastly increases the likelihood that you or your passengers will be killed or permanently disabled in even the most minor of collisions. Air bags are designed to work in conjunction with a seat belt and shoulder harness (when available), not alone. While it could be argued that there may have been a very few chance occurrences where a vehicle occupant survived because he or she was not restrained, those are usually random occurrences, and there are an overwhelmingly greater number of accidents where occupants would have survived had they been restrained.

Wunchai Intararit/123RF

Size, Mass and Maneuverability: It is generally easier to maneuver a small vehicle than a large one. Large vehicles such as half-ton (referring to its payload capacity) pick-up trucks can weigh 5000 to

8500 pounds or more. Conversely the average car weighs about 3000-4000 pounds. While it may seem that you would be safer in a larger pick-up or SUV, this may not always be the case. Trucks and SUV's have higher centers-of-gravity making them more prone to a rollover. Rollovers can be caused anytime the vehicle begins to move sideways due to slipping or skidding, or when over-controlling during aggressive maneuvering or swerving to avoid an accident. They can also occur after hitting something. And while only about 3% of single-vehicle accidents are rollover related, they result in about 30% of single-vehicle crash fatalities. Conversely, drivers of cars with lower centers-of-gravity can defensively maneuver more aggressively without as much risk of a rollover.

Many rollovers are caused by "over-correcting" when maneuvering. A driver may do this while avoiding another vehicle, or an animal or debris in the road. Over-correcting can also occur when a distracted driver drives off the road surface, only to swerve back onto the road and then lose control. Most of the time, having high situational awareness could have prevented this situation, for a variety of reasons. A driver with high SA is less likely to leave his or her lane or drive off the road surface in the first place. He or she is aware of other vehicles in the vicinity, can see road debris further ahead, and can plan to avoid surprises or aggressive maneuvering. A driver with high SA is also less likely to act impulsively to make a last-minute exit or lane change, or to succumb to startle upon leaving the road surface.

Performance and Power: Too much as well as too little performance can be problematic for a driver. Too much power misused can cause loss of control. Under excessive power, the rear wheels of a rear-wheel-drive car can slide out causing the car to veer off its intended course. Unfortunately, the intuitive response to this situation, which is to hit the brakes, will hamper controllability. Braking puts more weight on the front tires, and less on the rear tires when you need rear tire traction the most. Race car drivers know this tendency very well. Ironically, since their vehicles generate aerodynamic down force, these drivers know to brake early going into a turn when speed and down force are higher. Our vehicles are not designed the same way; we don't have the benefit of aerodynamic down force and must be more careful at higher speeds.

An under-powered vehicle can also be dangerous if the driver does not plan accordingly. For instance, an underpowered vehicle may not be able to accelerate to a safe road or highway speed before merging into traffic, or otherwise accelerate out of a predicament when necessary. This can increase the potential for a collision. As always, maintaining high SA, so that you can plan early, can offset some of these disadvantages.

Field-of-View (FOV) Limitations: Field-of-View (FOV) is the extent of the observable world that you can see at any given moment. While driving, there are obstructions to your vision from the structure of the vehicle. You, of course, also have physical limitations in your ability to move or rotate your body to look rearward. These visual obstructions and limitations decrease your ability to see the world around you. Mirrors enhance rearward FOV. Since maintaining high situational awareness is a visually intensive task, it pays to know your vehicle's FOV limitations and blind spots. Please take the time to set your vehicle up properly for safe driving and to minimize blind spots. To maximize your ability to clear behind you, ensure that your side view mirrors are adjusted far enough out on each side.

Leonid Dorfman/123RF

One technique is to lean into the driver side window and then adjust the driver side mirror outward until just before the side of your vehicle disappears in the mirror. Likewise, to adjust the passenger side mirror, lean over the center console of your vehicle, then adjust that that mirror outward until just before the other side of your vehicle disappears in the mirror. Unless you are planning to scan for flies stuck to the side of your car, it is of no value to see your car in your side-view mirrors. I do not necessarily adjust my mirrors as far outward as just stated in the above technique. But I do ensure that, for an approaching vehicle either side, I have visual overlap of those vehicles in the rearview and either side mirrors. For some reason, it is comforting to see the side of your vehicle in your side mirrors, but the more of your car you can see, the less you can see into your potential blind spots left and right.

As just implied, your driver side mirror would be set so that, before a vehicle approaching in the lane to your left (assuming right-hand driving rules and driver on the left of the vehicle) disappears completely in your front rearview mirror, you would start to see a portion of that vehicle come into view in your driver side mirror. Of course, this does not replace briefly looking rearward and to the left to clear for traffic when safe to do so. This is especially important when you are merging onto a freeway from an onramp. Due to the converging angle between the onramp and the freeway, you cannot always rely on your mirrors to detect traffic in the lane into which you will be merging. For the same reason, if you are established in your lane, and a vehicle is changing lanes from the left and behind into your lane, you may not see that vehicle if you rely solely on your mirrors, since that traffic is approaching you at an angle. Therefore, to be courteous of other drivers, you should avoid their blind spots as much as practical when you are aft of them and are moving into a lane adjacent to them. For instance, if you decide to change into the lane to your right, you should either wait until you are clear of the blind spot of any vehicle further to your right and ahead in the lane adjacent to the lane you want to move into, or just be extra cautious in doing so. In heavy traffic, that vehicle to your right may not know that you have merged into his or her blind spot and decide to cross into your lane and into you. It is, of course, that driver's responsibility to clear his or her blind spot, but you can help avoid

No driving blind
in the blind
spots.

an accident by being predictable and courteous. The same clearing guidelines that apply when clearing left, generally apply when clearing to the right as well.

Merging Drivers: Speaking of merging, it is, in most locations in the world, the responsibility of the merging driver to clear the lane and merge safely. There are some places where it is a joint responsibility of the merging driver and drivers already on the highway. Of course, regardless of rules, drivers on the highway should be courteous, safety conscious, and attempt to facilitate smooth merging of traffic. Nothing is worse than an un-courteous driver. However, many merging drivers apparently do not know how to merge properly, often attempting to merge well below the highway speed limit, and waiting until the merge lane ends to turn their signal on and merge. This behavior could be indicative of not clearing properly because of laziness or distraction. When you are merging into traffic, please be mindful of larger, less maneuverable vehicles such as semi-trucks and vehicles towing trailers. These vehicles are less maneuverable than you and their drivers are relying on you to plan your merge to avoid being a conflict to them. Do not expect them to move over for you. Bad drivers are the nemesis of these larger vehicles.

Problems with merging can also be due to drivers' inexperience or lack of confidence. These drivers are not sure who is in the highway lane or how close they are, because they either are not effectively scanning, they are not experienced enough to assess distance and closure properly, or they are just overly conservative. They therefore hesitate to merge. A confident driver with high SA will communicate his or her intentions early by signaling, have cleared properly, will merge at or near highway speeds, and have established a primary and back up merge game plan. And if it does not work out because of heavy traffic or un-courteous drivers on the highway, then they do not merge. They will exit if that is an option, slow down looking for the next gap in the traffic, or possibly pull off on the shoulder—which they have cleared—while being smooth and predictable to other traffic.

You should be courteous to drivers who do not drive very well. Some drivers have slower reflexes. Some drivers have poorer vision. In the US, you can drive with 20/50 corrected vision (20/60 daytime only) with a restricted license. And although having only one functioning eye hampers depth perception because of monocular vision, the Motor Vehicle Administration will allow you to drive if you have shown adequate visual acuity and field of view. Other drivers are limited in mobility and have a difficult time physically looking behind them. And some drivers are just overly cautious. Again, be courteous and compassionate.

Your Vehicle's Maintenance Status: Is your car well maintained? The right answer would be yes, but we are human, live on a budget, and are sometimes just plain neglectful or forgetful when it comes to our automobiles.

Old or broken windshield wipers can prevent you from seeing well in rain or snow. Burned out, dim, or misaligned headlights can prevent you from seeing far enough ahead at night. Inoperative headlights or taillights can also prevent other drivers from seeing you or adequately judging your distance from them. Drivers expect to see a pair of headlights or taillights, not just one. It is much more difficult for other drivers to judge their distance from you if you only have one head- or taillight working. This may cause them to turn in

dashadima/123RF

front of you or not be able to stop behind you. Inoperative brake lights on both sides of a vehicle or trailer are especially dangerous. Since motorcycles have only one head- and taillight, it is harder for other drivers to judge their distance at night. There are other vehicle problems that can get you into more trouble.

A steering system failure is another maintenance problem that could cause an accident, especially if the steering locks up. Although it is rare for a steering system to lock up while driving (assuming you do

[handwritten margin note: up loose obj in true seat onj's drive]

not turn the ignition key to the off/lock position), a more common problem is a power steering failure. This makes your vehicle much more difficult to steer, especially if you are driving a large vehicle.

Rarely, mechanical failures—sometimes due to poor design—can cause a sudden unintended acceleration. Also, a floor mat or other loose object can slide, or roll, forward and jam the accelerator. There is a right and wrong way out of this and it pays to know before it happens. In the event of an unintended acceleration or inability to reduce engine power, many drivers would turn off the ignition. Unfortunately, this will disable power steering, decrease braking effectiveness and potentially lock the steering wheel. The right thing to do would be to apply brakes, shift into neutral (automatic or manual transmission) and steer to the shoulder, or other safe location, and stop. At that point, you could turn off the ignition and shift to park or, with a manual transmission, set the parking brake. A panicking driver may not think to shift into neutral.

Tires: For something you may not pay too much attention to, or really understand, tires can be your best friend or worst nightmare on the road. Worn treads can cause loss of traction due to hydroplaning on a wet surface. Unfortunately, hydroplaning may occur on all tires simultaneously, effectively making your vehicle momentarily uncontrollable. If you are lucky, you may notice subtle loss of steering effectiveness, or a feeling like you are gliding across the road surface, soon enough to slow carefully and regain control before it becomes necessary to turn or brake heavily, which you would not be able to do if you were still hydroplaning.

Tires can fail or blow out because of a puncture from debris on the road. But they can also fail if worn excessively, or if they are just old. Tire failure can cause you to lose control of your vehicle. Overinflated tires can blowout. Underinflated tires can also cause early tire failure, especially if the vehicle is overloaded. In fact, underinflated tires blow out more often than overinflated tires. Underinflated tires can also aggravate hydroplaning. Old tires can blowout as well even if properly inflated and with good tread. One source recommends replacing tires more than five or six years old, no matter what the tread depth. Rubber gets old and dry rots, and even though the tire tread looks good, the tire may be in bad shape.

What do you do if you have a blowout? Probably not what you think. Just as a pilot will probably do the wrong thing in a severe overbanked nose low upset (closer to inverted than upright) if not trained properly, so will you possibly do the wrong thing if surprised by a tire blowout if you were not at least already aware of the proper procedure, to be discussed shortly.

Regarding tire inflation, the maximum tire pressure listed on your tire is the maximum cold pressure recommended for your tire to carry its maximum load (and should be measured when the vehicle has been driven less than a mile and the tire has not been sitting in the hot sun). It is a maximum pressure for the tire in general; the optimum tire pressure for those tires mounted on your specific vehicle is usually lower, and is recommended by your vehicle manufacturer. In newer vehicles, the recommended tire pressure is located on a sticker on the driver's door jam. Otherwise it can be found in the vehicle's owner's manual.

For a given tire pressure, increasing vehicle load will cause the tire to flatten slightly on the road surface. This will increase friction and heating. If the tire is underinflated for the load, this could cause early tire failure. Generally, for tires to carry more load, tire pressure should be increased (not decreased as many people think). Many accidents have occurred due to tire blowouts, because drivers have overloaded their trucks and SUV's on already underinflated and neglected tires.

Does this mean you should increase tire pressure when carrying heavier loads? Not necessarily. Remember, overinflated tires can cause early tire failure just as underinflated tires can. The recommended tire inflation pressure for your vehicle assumes that you are carrying the maximum recommended payload for that vehicle. So, you are safe if you always inflate your tires to their recommended pressure (check frequently) and never overload your vehicle. There may be additional recommendations for adjusting tire pressure when towing or carrying heavier loads. Drivers who transition from light loads to heavy loads (for instance, when towing a camper or loading the bed of a pickup with heavy loads) can refer to load and inflation tables for their vehicle.

Critical Action Procedures: While we are discussing tire blowouts, let's introduce an important concept of operating complex vehicles in a complex environment (that's you operating your vehicle in day-to-day driving) — Critical Action Procedures or CAPs. In the aviation community, pilots are trained to deal with many different emergency conditions. In many of these emergencies, pilots have at least a fair amount of time to reference the emergency checklist, to troubleshoot the problem, and perhaps to evaluate alternative courses of action. However, there are some emergency procedures

that require memorization and action without reference to a checklist. This is because they are either extremely time critical or happen in a phase of flight where the pilot or crew cannot divert their attention from flying the aircraft, such as when low to the ground during takeoff or landing. I'll call these time-critical emergency procedures "Critical Action Procedures" or CAPs. That is what we call them in the F-16 fighter community and I think it is applicable here. Multi-crew aircraft have QRH's (Quick Reference Handbooks) for the "pilot monitoring" (the pilot not flying) to reference while the pilot flying flies the aircraft.

Even during the worst of emergencies such as loss-of-control in-flight, where a flight crew may find their aircraft upside down nose low and accelerating rapidly, the flight crew typically has a few seconds to initiate effective procedures to recover their aircraft safely. When driving, consider the fact that you are sometimes driving only feet from other vehicles in your lane and adjacent lanes, and from obstacles on the edge of the road. The next time you drive next to a 75,000-pound tractor trailer, realize that its driver could possibly lose control if one of the front steering tires blows out. A truck tire could blow out right next to you, or disintegrate, sending debris in your direction. And if your own vehicle's tire blows out, your vehicle could go off the road or contact another vehicle in a second or two. You are, when driving, in an environment as critical as a pilot rotating his aircraft on takeoff, where experiencing a critical emergency requires split second decision making. This is not a big deal only if you drive prepared for the worst, and drive aware – meaning NOT distracted. Pilots rehearse emergency situations over and over in the simulator. Drivers usually do not have access to such training, and are just not trained to handle crises on the road because crises do not often very often. But as in flying, it is the uncommon event where most fatalities occur. This holds true in driving.

A tire blowout, for instance, is uncommon, but the stakes are very high. I have had two or three tire blowouts in my 37 years of driving due to punctures from small road debris. In each case the outcome was uneventful, but only for several specific reasons. I do not drive distracted. I know who is around me. In my 37 years of flying, I have trained for far worse scenarios. I have also been taught to not panic, and to always maintain control of my vehicle during an emergency. The best way to maintain control is to pay attention when driving, be ready for a crisis, and never let yourself lose control of your vehicle in the first place.

Maneuvering Awareness: Because drivers are typically not trained to handle critical vehicle emergencies, I would highly recommend that you take an advanced driving course. Such a course could reteach you basic driving habits like vehicle set up (e.g. seats and mirrors). It could also teach you advanced driving skills such as how to handle a skid, how to perform maximum braking, how to maneuver to avoid an accident without over-controlling, how to

Sergey Pykhonin /123RF

drive in slippery road conditions, how to maintain high SA, etc. Some courses can teach you how to handle an actual tire blowout. A high-performance driving course with a racing school would provide you with driving skills in a racing context which would also make you a safer driver. Such a course would not teach you to drive fast and recklessly on the road. Professional race car drivers, like professional pilots, practice the utmost in discipline. A racing course would teach you how to recognize the performance limit of a vehicle in a crisis or during poor road conditions, how to perform threshold braking, etc. It would make you more aware of how to keep from losing control in a crisis. If approached correctly, such a course would teach you the importance of discipline when driving.

Recognition-Primed Decision Making (RPD): One advantage of taking an advanced driving course is that it can enable you to react faster and more automatically in a crisis. Human beings make decisions in different ways. The most familiar way is when we recognize a need to act, evaluate alternative courses of action (e.g. action "A," "B," or "C"); and then finally decide on the best course of action. This process is time consuming, however, and may be inadequate in a time-critical complex environment, where perhaps making a quick decision can mean the difference between life and death. In this environment, action must be immediate. There is little time to evaluate alternative courses of action. Here, it is better to make an adequate, if less than ideal, decision and act quickly, than to waste time to come up with an ideal course of action. This type of decision making is called recognition-primed decision making or RPD.

Whether you are a driver, pilot, firefighter, emergency medical provider, someone walking to your car at night in a parking lot, a jogger in a park, or anyone else who may have to act quickly in a crisis, training can accelerate the process of RPD. For example, in a personal self-defense hands-on training program, you are placed in realistic scenarios where you learn to recognize visual, auditory, tactile (touch) and other sensory cues that trigger you to react quickly and decisively in a certain way. You are also taught to engage in a "what-if" analysis in each environment that you find yourself in—before a crisis occurs. Here you ask yourself, what could go wrong in each phase of a given activity and what would you do about it. You are also taught to have high situational awareness and to be ready, perhaps with car keys placed in your hand to be used as a weapon if someone attacks you in a parking lot. When sensory cues in a real-world environment indicate certain matching patterns experienced in training, you can then react much more quickly and automatically while overcoming startle and suppressing panic (If you are thinking, "I cannot do any of this while driving if I am on my cell phone or daydreaming," you are exactly right).

Sensory pattern matching gets the ball rolling…it gets you moving and acting decisively. Sensory pattern matching means that, in a real-world situation, if you recognize sensory cues (visual, auditory, touch, smell) from a previously encountered situation (either from training or an actual event), that are indicative of a developing or actual crisis, you can then react immediately to take control of the situation. You recognize the crisis, and choose the first acceptable (not necessarily the most ideal) decision or action. Once the ball is rolling towards an acceptable solution, you can continue to engage in level 1, 2, and 3 SA and modify your actions appropriately. But at least you move towards a safe, acceptable, lifesaving solution immediately.

These immediate RPD responses bypass what is considered normal and time-permissive responses, and they must be trained, ingrained and well thought out. Human Factors researchers would call such RPD responses "naturalistic" decision making, meaning how humans can realistically react in a time-critical, demanding situation, versus how traditional research has dictated that we should respond, which is by always taking time to evaluate alternative courses of action and then taking time to choose the best one. RPD means immediate and proper action versus delayed response, while hopefully avoiding impulsive and improper reaction, or even inaction, due to startle or panic.

It is possible that decision making can proceed directly and rapidly from a recognized situation such as a nose low overbanked upset while flying, or a tire blowout while driving – and then to predefined actions with a high level of automaticity. This is a classic "fight like you train" example. In this environment, efficient (not necessarily ideal) action is paramount.

In the flying environment, an example of recognition-primed decision making might be a scenario where the aircraft is tossed by another aircraft's wake turbulence into a severely overbanked attitude (closer to upside down than right-side-up), low to the ground. In this example, a properly trained pilot would immediately unload on the controls (push slightly) and initiate an aggressive roll upright. Unloading lessens altitude loss and makes the aircraft roll more quickly back to upright, yet it's a very unnatural response and must be learned through repetitive hands-on training. The pilot can then begin a pull to avoid the ground but only when the aircraft is closer to upright. The pilot's initial RPD response of pushing and rolling using up to maximum roll rate while severely overbanked would be better than pulling back, pulling and rolling, or not rolling aggressively enough, all of which are unfortunately the instinctive untrained—and potentially deadly—responses in this situation.

An example of RPD in the driving environment would be the calm, controlled and immediate reaction necessary when a tire blows out. In this case, the driver could preserve momentum by tapping the accelerator if necessary, to maintain control, stay in the lane, and avoid immediate braking or swerving, then steer towards a shoulder.

Such a response could be mastered through hands-on training such as learned in an advanced driving course. There are also driving simulators that can better prepare you to react immediately in a crisis. In general, the more repetitive the training, the better. Accomplishing this training is not always practical for the average driver. If you have not had this type of training, your chances of success in a such a crisis can be maximized by knowing what an acceptable life-saving response to the crisis is before it occurs, by maintaining a high level of situational awareness, by having the mindset that you will always maintain control of your vehicle, and by avoiding panic and over control.

The more complete your mental model of the driving domain to include how to react in a crisis, the less interpretation and delay in decision-making you must do in a driving crisis; just as the more complete the mental model of aircraft upset recovery a pilot has, the less interpretation and decision making the pilot must do in an actual upset situation. If you always drive distracted, you will be woefully unprepared for a true driving crisis. Rest assured, even if you don't participate in an advanced maneuvering course, being alert, and undistracted, with high SA, and with knowledge of what can go wrong, and the basics of how to deal with it, all will still afford you a greater chance of success in dealing with your next big driving crisis.

Driving CAPs: Regardless of whether you participate in an advanced driving or racing course, it would pay for you to memorize and contemplate some Critical Action Procedures (CAPs) for driving emergency situations that could kill you if you do not react quickly and by memory. As stated before, a tire blowout is one such CAP.

Caution: The following driving CAPs are suggestions only. What you do in a given situation depends on your vehicles systems, recommended procedures, your driving environment and your own experience and skills.

Akhararat Wathanasing/123RF

Tire Blowout: If you have a tire blowout, consider the following guidelines. Avoid immediate braking if practical. When you have a tire blowout, your vehicle settles and shifts in the direction of the blown tire, but the momentum of your vehicle tries to carry it in the direction it was going because of mass and inertia. For example, with a failed left front tire, your vehicle's nose veers left, and as it does, your vehicle still wants to go straight in a direction now right of the vehicle's centerline. Applying brakes may aggravate this tendency of your vehicle to veer in the opposite direction that it is going. When you experience a tire blowout, it is important not over-control or swerve. You have potentially lost 25% of your traction. Over-controlling can send you immediately sideways and out of control. This could cause a roll over, especially in a truck, SUV or other vehicle with a high center-of-gravity. Yet braking and swerving opposite the direction that your vehicle shifts are typical reactions of a startled or distracted driver who has not considered appropriate actions in this situation beforehand and suddenly finds him- or herself in a crisis. Add to these considerations the very likely probability that many drivers may not be aware of other vehicles around them (low SA), and may not even have their hands placed properly on the steering wheel—oversights that could severely hamper maintaining vehicle control.

Some driving experts suggest that the correct response in a typical blowout situation is opposite to what might be intuitive to most drivers. For instance, Mac Demere, who has taught over a thousand drivers to successfully control their vehicle after a tire blowout, suggests that drivers not do much initially…do not brake and do not swerve. Instead, maintain control and stay in your lane (the author suggests that you could allow your vehicle to gradually steer into the blown tire while maintaining positive control, but you do not want to hit anyone in the lane next to you). What do you do with your right foot? If your vehicle begins to swerve, you may want to press on the accelerator pedal gently to maintain momentum until you can guarantee control. This action may not be necessary, but it is certainly counterintuitive. There will be a lot of drag from the failed tire and your vehicle will want to decelerate which can cause it to become unstable. Tapping the accelerator will most likely not cause your vehicle to increase speed. At best, it will slow your rate of deceleration, keeping your vehicle stable until you can guarantee control.

tap accelerator? gently

Doing nothing with the accelerator pedal (neither accelerating nor coasting) might be the second-best initial action. But even taking your foot off the accelerator pedal to coast would be better than immediate braking. Of course, if you must brake to avoid an accident, then brake, but only as much as necessary. If you find it necessary to tap the accelerator to maintain control, then once you have guaranteed control, you can then ease off the accelerator, and begin steering gently towards the shoulder. It would be ideal to steer towards the shoulder on the side of the blown tire for two reasons. First, that is where your vehicle wants to go. Second, once you pull off, you want that tire that you must change to be on the side opposite traffic, which is a safer place to change a tire.

Of course, there will be times where steering toward the failed tire is impractical or unsafe. The time you have a blowout is not the time to determine that. If you have high SA, then you would already know where you should go—and where you can go. Do not immediately worry about the hazard light button unless you can activate it while keeping your eyes on the road. Be predictable so that other drivers can avoid you. The following could be considered a critical action procedure or CAP for a tire blowout. It does not in any way replace common sense given the context of the situation, or correct or recommended procedures by your vehicle manufacturer.

Suggested Tire Blowout CAPs:

1. Maintain positive control of your vehicle.

2. Avoid immediate braking or swerving, if practical, and remain predictable to other vehicles.

3. Consider tapping the accelerator pedal to maintain momentum until control is guaranteed.

4. Steer in a predictable and safe manner to the side of the road (the side of the blowout if practical).

5. Then let off the accelerator while maintaining control and brake gradually to a stop (do not steer onto shoulder at high speed unless safe to do so).

Ehsnils/commons.Wikimedia.org

Failed Brakes: Poor braking action or failed brakes is another dangerous vehicle maintenance problem: Brake problems can cause you to be unable to avoid an accident you could otherwise have avoided if they were working properly. If the brake warning light (usually red) illuminates, it could just mean one or more brakes are worn and must be replaced. It could mean low brake fluid level, compromising braking effectiveness. It could also indicate a problem with your ABS (anti-lock braking system; some vehicles have a separate ABS warning light). If your vehicle's brakes fail to the point at which your ability to stop safely is in jeopardy, consider following these procedures.

Brake failure: 1. ABS = firm hold brakes

Suggested Brake Failure CAPs:

1. To attempt to regain braking effectiveness, apply brakes firmly and hold if you have Antilock Braking System (ABS), or pump brakes firmly and repeatedly to attempt to build brake pressure if you do not have ABS.

2. Ensure your foot is off the accelerator, and downshift one gear at a time (manual or automatic) to slow.

3. If braking effectiveness is not regained, use parking brake handle to slow (if foot operated, gently depress but be ready to release if braking becomes excessive).

4. Steer towards a safe place (do not steer onto shoulder at high speed unless safe to do so).

5. Come to a stop, shift into neutral and set parking brake.

6. Note: Avoid turning off the engine until you are stopped, unless necessary, as this will disable power steering. If necessary to turn off the engine, avoid turning ignition all the way to off/lock as this will lock the steering wheel.

If you decide to drive a car with one or more critical systems poorly maintained, then do so at your own risk - adjust your driving habits accordingly, and don't put others' lives at risk. Stay off highways and heavily used roads, and avoid high speeds. If your brakes are "spongy" then increase your spacing on vehicles in front of you. If your tires have worn treads, or are underinflated, drive slowly and on secondary roads until you can fix the problem. But beware. It is in fact illegal to drive an automobile that is maintained below legal standards on public roads. You could be liable in the event of an accident. It is best to have your vehicle inspected at recommended intervals and to get your automobile to a repair shop if you know if, or suspect a problem. If it is not safe to drive the vehicle, have it towed to the nearest repair facility.

Vehicle Technology and Complacency: When relatively inexperienced aviators fly "technologically advanced aircraft" or TAA's, they tend to feel that they, and their machines, are more capable than they really are (the same complacency can occur with professional pilots flying sophisticated corporate jets and airliners, although those pilots are typically better trained). This is a normal, but dangerous, human behavior. Drivers tend to feel the same way, for instance, in higher performance vehicles with advanced instrumentation and sensors. Even motorcyclists will tell you that, when they wear protective riding suits, they tend to feel more confident - perhaps more invincible - on the road. Inexperienced pilots in advanced aircraft may even feel overconfident when flying in adverse conditions such as in and around thunderstorms. For instance, a pilot who flies with the latest autopilot and satellite weather and map displays can feel "cozy in the cockpit" despite thunder and lightning enveloping the aircraft. An aviator, no matter how experienced, is no more capable of surviving these extreme hazardous conditions just because he or she is flying an advanced aircraft. Experienced, disciplined aviators know how dangerous and lethal these conditions can be. They know that, whether they fly the lowest performance, most basically equipped light aircraft trainer, or a very sophisticated "decked out" fast prop or jet, flying through a severe thunderstorm could still kill them.

At the end of the day, all vehicles, from budget models to exotic cars, do basically the same thing – they get you from point A to point B. Some vehicles just look and feel better, and go faster. Most "high-tech" navigation, communication and entertainment systems are potentially lethal distractions no matter how they are used. Heads-up Displays (HUDs), discussed later, are perhaps one of the few current readily available technologies, either through OEM (original equipment manufacturer) or through aftermarket vendors, that can reduce distraction. Of course, this is only true to the extent that a HUD displays only essential SA enhancing information in the driver's forward field-of-view. Displaying entertainment or infotainment information in a HUD is just lessening the risk severity of an already existing unnecessary driving distraction, and less or none of that type of information regardless of where it is displayed is always better.

Other driver-centric technologies, which convey information directly to the driver to enhance SA and decision making, are changing rapidly for the better. Examples of such technologies include user selectable dashboard displays; high resolution and low light camera displays that can replace or augment rear-view mirrors, forward low light and night vision, rear view back-up cameras and sensors; and adaptive LED headlights. Emerging technologies such as vehicle-to-vehicle (V2V) communications (where vehicles communicate safety-enhancing information with each other), and vehicle-to-infrastructure (V2I or V2X) communications are being researched. These technologies will enhance driver SA directly, or work more autonomously depending on how the vehicle is configured. They can improve safety and traffic efficiency. In addition to driver SA-enhancing systems, are the active safety systems that work partly or wholly without driver intervention, such

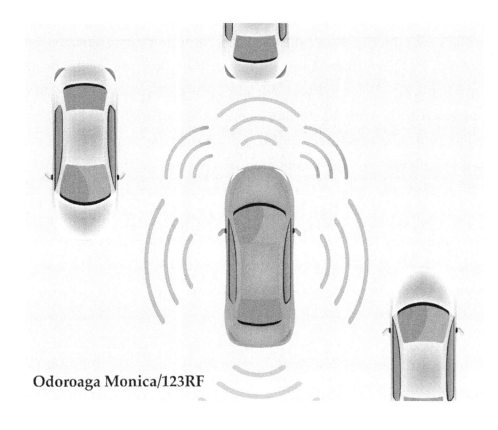

Odoroaga Monica/123RF

as vehicle collision avoidance, stability, braking, performance, and autonomous vehicle technology.

Until self-driving and autonomous vehicles take the driver out of the loop, most driver-centric technology, even safety or SA-enhancing technology, when used improperly, can be a potentially lethal distraction. Drivers cannot afford to fixate their attention on any one source of information for too long, at the expense of visual scanning forward of the vehicle and maintaining high situational awareness of other vehicles and road conditions in the immediate vicinity.

When flying, a pilot usually has a reasonable amount of time to assimilate traffic, terrain, and navigation chart information—not much unless flying on autopilot—but at least some time. After all, an aircraft is, most of the time, thousands of feet above the ground and under Air Traffic Control, providing traffic separation. On the road, the driver is literally just a few feet away from other vehicles and hazards. Even when using self-driving or "autopilot" systems, you should still spend a reasonable amount of time scanning for traffic and hazards in the driving environment. Automation may let you down, and it is wise to keep your SA high and be prepared to take over. Technology does not replace being prepared to drive so that you can minimize distraction on the road. One way to avoid distraction on the road is to engage in some pre-drive planning just as any responsible pilot engages in preflight planning. For instance, if you plan to drive an unfamiliar route, then it would be wise for you to become familiar with your route before you begin driving— despite sophisticated navigation systems in your vehicle. Being familiar with your route will minimize distraction from these navigation aids.

Wingmen Awareness: Certain specialty flying operations such as military aviation, coast guard, airborne fire suppression, aerial demonstration teams, all entail flying with your wingmen—other pilots in aircraft that support your mission. You train with them and you can trust them. They are there to support you and maximize mission success. Perhaps except for racing as a part of a team, or when driving with fellow club drivers, you are pretty much on your own when driving. You do not have "wingmen" in the classical sense. I mention this for a specific reason. It is very easy to trust other drivers on the road, especially when they appear to be driving responsibly and predictably. Unfortunately, you do not know them or their experience level, nor do you know their immediate state of distraction. While they may not be acting in an immediate, threatening fashion, even outwardly trustworthy drivers can let you down—intentionally or otherwise—in a heartbeat. Driving defensively and conservatively can help you avoid the pitfalls of having blind faith in drivers around you. For instance, it is wise to always assume that the driver ahead of you might stop suddenly, and to maintain a safe distance from that vehicle (not to mention that you are also at fault if you hit that vehicle). And any driver around you can swerve into your lane at any time, if not maliciously, perhaps just due to oversight. By the way, when you tailgate a driver in front of you (meaning you are within minimum safe and legal distance for your current speed under present road conditions) you are placing a lot of blind faith in that driver to remain predictable.

You do have wingmen on call in the driving environment. Police, state troopers, EMT, firefighters and other emergency responders are just a call away. Drive responsibly; don't put their lives—and the lives of others—unnecessarily at risk on the road, respect what they do for you, and they will be there for you.

Navigation Awareness: Navigation awareness is the awareness of your location "on the map." It is an understatement to say that, when you drive, you typically want to know where you are on the surface of the Earth. To go for a leisurely scenic drive, to get lost and not care about where you are, is a rare luxury. Most often, you must keep up with where you are at any given time so that you can navigate to wherever it is you have chosen as your destination. Navigation aids such as voice assisted vehicle GPS systems or the assisted-GPS technology in your smart phone, when used properly, can be minimally distracting. You should, however, be aware of local laws governing use of these devices. GPS devices are strictly covered under distracted driving laws.

ARISTICCO LLC/123RF

Physically holding a phone or other GPS device while driving will almost always get you into trouble. And mounting a portable device on the windshield is illegal in over half of U.S. states. It is a good idea to set up navigation in your GPS before you drive; or have a passenger do it for you. Minimize visual distraction by only glancing briefly at a time at the display. When listening to voice commands, minimize cognitive distraction by placing priority on safe driving over navigation commands—even if you are about to miss your exit, or do not fully understand a command. Never let a GPS command or queue cause you to maneuver unsafely, or without high SA. Just because you have this technology, does not mean that you can afford to be lulled into a sense of complacency or, on the other hand, a false sense of urgency.

Aviators learn the following priorities: "Aviate, Navigate, Communicate." For you that means, "Drive, Navigate, Communicate." Anything that causes you to be distracted from visual scanning and anything that increases your mental workload will detract from your driving SA. To be clear, using navigation devices will increase your positional SA, but such activity may decrease the SA that will keep you alive. It is great to know where you are or where you must go, but if you crash while trying to determine that information, then it will only help you to steer emergency responders to the scene of your accident.

majivecka/123RF

Spatial Awareness: Spatial awareness is an awareness of how your body is oriented and located in three-dimensional space. An example of spatial awareness is the ability of a gymnast, who performs a complicated gymnastic routine including balance, aerial, cartwheel and other moves, to continuously maintain a keen overall sense of not only body orientation with respect to upright, but also of physical location in space with respect to the height above the mat, and to the edge of the mat. Motocross, ski, and skateboard acrobats, divers, and aerobatic pilots must also have a developed 3-D spatial awareness.

In general, to know how you are oriented in three-dimensional space requires a variety of different senses including your visual, proprioceptive, kinesthetic, and vestibular senses. Proprioception is the sense of the relative position of your head, arms, and legs, etc. It relies on proprioceptors or sensors located in your muscles, joints and fascia (fascia is elastic internal connective tissue that wraps around your organs, providing support, connecting layers of muscle, and surrounds all your internal body tissues). Complementing proprioception is a kinesthetic awareness of your spatial location and orientation (pilots call this a "seat-of-the-pants" awareness). Your vestibular system includes components of the inner ear that sense rotational movement (the semicircular canal) and linear acceleration (the otolith organ). The vestibular system provides a sense of balance and spatial orientation for the purpose of coordinating movement with balance. Your brain combines visual, proprioceptive, and vestibular inputs along with your kinesthetic awareness, to determine overall sense of body position, movement and acceleration.

When you actively use your vision, you can maintain an accurate sense of your orientation and position in three-dimensional space. The previously mentioned acrobats are not always looking where they are going while tumbling through the air; therefore, they must have a very high level of SA on where they are, in what direction they are headed, and where they can anticipate ending up the next time they are looking in that direction.

Airplanes can fly in any attitude in three-dimensional space, although pilots desire to keep their machines, at least the ones carrying passengers, within narrow pitch and bank parameters. Pilots must maintain 3-D spatial awareness to maintain control of their aircraft, or to regain control if the aircraft deviates from acceptable parameters. Except for aerobatic, air show, and military fighter pilots, and pilots like me who like to be upside-down to teach all the other pilots how to get right-side-up, being other than upright is, of course, typically a very undesirable state for a pilot and aircraft to be in. To avoid deviating from some semblance of upright, or to recover back towards upright if necessary, the pilot must have an accurate spatial awareness, provided by visual interpretation of actual or instrument horizon references. Visual scanning is the primary way to determine attitude when flying. When driving, visual scanning is the primary way to determine position on the road surface as well as where one is headed. The other senses including the vestibular system can deceive a pilot or driver who is visually distracted.

At least in terms of 3-dimensional spatial awareness, driving is not nearly as complicated as flying or tumbling through the air—unless you are jumping the Grand Canyon in a rocket powered car—so you might easily assume that it would be no problem to keep your bearings spatially on a road surface if visually distracted for a mere few seconds. After all, you must only deal with the two horizontal dimensions when driving. Unfortunately, as simple as the task of spatial orientation is while driving, a driver is only able to reliably determine position on the road surface, as well as detect any developing deviations from the lane, if that driver continuously scans the environment. During the time that you look down at a GPS display, or a phone, or somewhere other than where you are going, you rely solely on your memory of where you just were, and of where you were headed the moment you looked away. You may believe that you can rely on your non-visual senses (your vestibular and seat-of-the-pants senses) to help you stay in your lane. But that is just not the case. Also, during the short time you look away, you are making the risky assumption that traffic and other hazards will remain predictable (for instance, the car in front of you will not brake suddenly or a truck tire won't disintegrate near you) for the duration your visual attention is diverted. Your peripheral vision may detect a hazard, but this is less likely if you are cognitively focused on something inside the car.

The most fundamental oversight here is that a driver thinks he or she can keep a vehicle straight by "feel" alone. Within the aviation domain, it has been proven time and time again that pilots lack completely, the combined proprioceptive, kinesthetic, and vestibular capability to keep their aircraft upright by feel alone. In fact, airline pilots get to experience a "vestibular sub-threshold" roll in the simulator while visually distracted. This exercise involves an insidious roll into a significant bank angle at a roll rate below the threshold of the human vestibular system (approximately 2.5 to 5 degrees per second). Below this threshold of roll rate, a pilot's vestibular system will not detect the increasing bank angle developing. If a pilot manually flying an airplane (not on autopilot) looks away from a horizon reference for more than a few moments, it is probable that his aircraft will begin to diverge from a wings level attitude. Professional pilots are therefore trained not to divert their attention away from the attitude reference for more than a very brief moment when manually flying the aircraft...ever. Even when on autopilot, they are frequently crosschecking their attitude and monitoring the performance of the autopilot and other systems. And this is considering that the typical pilot has far more training preparing to become a pilot than the typical driver has had preparing for a simple driving test.

Ironically, that GPS moving map in your vehicle that was designed to keep you "in the know" as to where you are on the map, can, if used improperly, completely let you down from a spatial awareness standpoint. Truth is, from the second you are distracted from the road, you have lost your local spatial awareness as well as your ability to see crises developing that require immediate attention. One of the quickest ways to lose spatial awareness is to look and reach towards the back seat, for instance, to reach for something, or to help a child in a car seat behind you. In this case, as discussed earlier but worth mentioning again, you remove your eyes from the road, including your peripheral vision; you rotate your head, which may introduce vestibular disorientation and cause vertigo in extreme cases; and you twist your torso, which can increase the likelihood of introducing an erroneous input on the steering wheel.

You may think that you can sense your position on the road while diverting your attention. Your vehicle may begin immediately deviating from your lane and you will not sense it, a vehicle in front

Don't look away!!!

of you could slam on the brakes, or a piece if debris unseen to you could come through your windshield. When not engaging proactively in maintaining high SA by continuously scanning, your SA diminishes rapidly in the dynamic environment of driving. When you divert your vision or mental focus to a diversionary task, you could be a second or two away from disaster. Visual distractions from the road ahead must be limited to extremely brief periods of time, a half second to a second perhaps, to guarantee safety.

Environmental Elements: Traffic, Road, Obstacles, Weather

Environmental Awareness: This is an awareness of the various elements within your local environment that require attention. In the driving domain, these elements include other vehicles, of course, to which you devote most of your immediate attention. Other elements include, but are not limited to, road surface and condition, signage, condition of road shoulders, debris on the road surface, obstacles in and on the side of the road, weather hazards and trends, road curvature and design; anything external to you and your machine.

Assessing Traffic: You must pay constant attention to other vehicles. They are arguably, second to distraction, the biggest threat to your safety. Assessing traffic includes estimating the location of other vehicles relative to you, their distance, and relative speed or closure (closure means the rate at which vehicles are "closing" or getting closer to you; it is your relative speed or speed difference with respect to another vehicle). It is, for instance, a good idea to be aware of larger vehicles behind and around you in stop and go, rush hour traffic. Knowing that a large vehicle behind you will have more difficulty stopping should tell you to increase your spacing on the vehicle in front of you. Doing so allows you to be more predictable and to slow more gradually giving the vehicle behind you more time to slow down. For "graduate level SA," always look for an "out"—a place to maneuver clear of your lane—in unpredictable traffic (construction, adverse weather), for instance, when a large truck is behind you; in case the driver of that truck cannot stop behind you. Again, distraction will prevent you from doing this effectively. You should also increase your distance from the vehicle in front of you when being tailgated for the same reason. Perhaps the tailgater will "get the message" and move on. It is also wise to pick out unpredictable or erratic drivers and stay away from them. Move over if they want to pass. Report them to the police, but do not get in their way. Don't brake check a driver behind you. Intentional tailgaters won't learn their lesson this way, and it may cause an accident or make you the victim of road rage.

Traffic is not a collection of individual vehicles so much as it is a living, breathing, dynamic collection of drivers in their vehicles. You should always consider your actions in traffic. Are you helping or hurting the flow of traffic? You should always drive in such a manner as to facilitate smooth efficient movement. It is not about you (an immature attitude for sure); but selfish, arrogant people tend to be selfish, arrogant drivers. For instance, when traffic changes speed, you should adjust your spacing accordingly. As it slows, you decrease your distance on the vehicle ahead. As speed increases, increase your distance. You should never be closer than a safe distance. On the other hand, you should not be "that guy" who, especially in slow moving or stopped traffic, maintains more than a reasonable distance behind traffic ahead (given considerations mentioned in the previous paragraph). Consider what would happen if everyone did that. Then a 10-mile long traffic jam would be 30 miles long; and would be a lot slower, and more painful. A driver might maintain excess spacing because of anxiety or poor vision. But when it is due to distraction or taking fuel economy to the extreme, it is a mark of self-serving attitude at the expense of all other drivers.

Once you become an experienced driver, it becomes easier to predict what other drivers are going to do before they do it. For instance, you may sense that the driver in front of you and in the lane to your left is positioning to merge into your lane. Call it a sixth sense (discussed later), but it is merely your ability in this case to match that driver's behavior with your own behavior and expectations. If you do not know what I am talking about then you are either new to driving or spend too much time distracted to learn the art of driving well.

Weather: Weather hazards do not get the attention from us that they deserve. I have driven on Arizona highways in such severe conditions that authorities recommended staying off the road unless it was urgent to do otherwise (yes, I just called myself out). It is easy to feel that you are protected from harm in your vehicle. Environmental forces far less severe than a tornado can still be very hazardous. Hail can damage your vehicle. Relatively shallow flood waters in a road dip can carry a vehicle away. Water just two feet deep can float a car or bus. Slippery road conditions can render your vehicle uncontrollable. High winds may not be so dangerous, but the heavy tree or power lines that come toppling down on your car because of those winds can be deadly; and so can flying debris that could smash through your windshield. High winds can also topple a large truck; bad for the truck driver—and for you, if you are next to that truck.

ambrozinio/123RF

Heavy rain, smoke, or fog can make the road and traffic ahead invisible. The next time you consider that it would be easy to just pull over upon entering these conditions, look at the statistics. Driving into severely reduced visibility conditions significantly increases your chances of being hit by another vehicle, and is one of the quickest ways to get into the middle of a pile up. Doing so might be analogous to a low time, non-instrument trained pilot who inadvertently flies into the weather, thus statistically shortening his life span to two minutes. If you anticipate low or no visibility conditions ahead due to fog, blowing dust, smoke, or extremely heavy rain, it is best to exit or turn off the road and take an alternate route, or wait until conditions improve before resuming driving.

If you inadvertently enter such conditions, find a place to exit the road completely while you can still see. Otherwise pull over as far off the road as possible and immediately turn your lights off so someone behind you does not attempt to follow you, potentially causing that driver to plow into the back of your vehicle. Regarding poor weather and road conditions, it is important to consider that, even if you feel prepared, other drivers sharing the road with you may not be so prepared.

Threat Awareness: Threats to your safety on the road come in many different forms. While all drivers may be potential threats, erratic or aggressive drivers are active threats and you should get out of their way. While you can and should report them, do not try to prove a point or teach them a lesson on the road. Other threats to your safety include debris in the road and flying debris such as rocks and chunks of rubber tire thrown from other vehicles. Small debris on the road surface tends to accumulate on and around lane boundaries, gores and shoulders since it is gradually pushed there by traffic. Given that truck tires are more apt to sling rocks into the air and into your path, you should be especially careful when a truck is changing lanes in front of you. Its tires are more likely to pick up and sling debris that has accumulated at the lane boundary.

Have you ever thought about how dangerous it is to remain next to a large semi, dump or cement truck while driving? Two things can happen. If the truck needs to swerve to avoid something; or if it hits something and swerves, your vehicle and you could literally be crushed. Also, what would happen if a truck tire disintegrated right in front of you or next to you? A large truck tire could blow out with enough force to knock a small car off the road. This is not to say that you should do something unsafe to avoid trucks, just don't loiter next to them. Pass them safely or remain clear. They don't want you to hang around them either. Of course, do not loiter left and behind them either. The lane to the left is for passing. If you are not going to pass, move into the lane behind the truck, and remain at a safe distance. Don't hang out it the left lane.

Temporal (Time) Awareness: Temporal awareness is an awareness of the passage of time and of the effect of time on elements in your driving domain. As an example, if you look in your review mirror and see a faster vehicle approaching in the lane to your left, you may decide to wait to change lanes until the vehicle passes. Whether you wait or not depends on your spatial awareness of that vehicle—how far away it is from you—and your temporal awareness of how quickly that vehicle will become a factor to you if you change lanes now. Through experience, you learn to judge distance as well as closure accurately.

Your ability to accurately assess the change in time of vehicle

Check the opp. turn lanes when turning on to a road.

location and of other elements in the driving domain becomes more complicated as more variables are introduced. This is especially true in a time critical environment, such as when attempting to pass someone on a two-lane road with approaching traffic in the opposing lane. In this case, you must not only judge your passing maneuver time—the time it will take you to pass the vehicle in front of you and reenter your lane—but you must also judge the distance and closure of the vehicle approaching in the opposing lane to ensure that you can complete the pass before the opposing traffic enters your passing range and becomes a collision hazard. Experience will allow you to estimate distance, closure and passing time, but the vehicle in the opposing lane could be going faster than your experience and SA tell you it is going, which would complicate your assessment. Inexperienced drivers have a more difficult time judging distance and closure problems and must drive more conservatively. *She can't tell closure*

When you drive distracted, your temporal awareness deteriorates along with all other aspects of your SA. Further, any driver can be confounded in infrequently encountered situations. The unusually large number of vehicle and pedestrian near misses and accidents with trains is a good example of this. It is difficult for vehicle drivers and pedestrians to judge train distance and closure because they have relatively little experience in doing so. Operating in a predicable manner is important for any vehicle operator or pedestrian in the transportation network.

An example of the importance of predictability is when pedestrians and bicyclists cross at crosswalks. A vehicle driver has a much more

105

difficult task predicting the future location of a pedestrian running, or bicyclist riding across a cross walk. Pedestrians should walk predictably through cross walks. Even if it is legal to run across a crosswalk or pedestrian crossing, you are making the motorist's job of avoiding you more difficult, especially if you change direction suddenly and dart across the cross walk. Bicyclists should walk their bikes across crosswalks, assuming they are using the crosswalk and not sharing the road with other drivers. A bicyclist walking his or her bike has all the rights and privileges of any pedestrian. But when bicyclists are on their bikes and their feet leave the ground, they are no longer pedestrians and must abide by the same laws that apply to vehicle drivers (of course there are still privileges granted exclusively to bicyclists depending on the state or country in which they ride). As a vehicle driver, you should be empathetic to pedestrians, bicyclists and motorcycle riders. They are very vulnerable to your actions. But if you are a pedestrian, bicyclist or motorcycle rider, you should act defensively, knowing that heavier vehicles can ruin you day.

CHAPTER SIX: THE SENSES AND PERCEPTION

semisatch/123RF

Human Perception: Driving is, as stated earlier, obviously a very visually-intensive task. The other senses are important as well, and it is worth some time to look at human perception in general, and its limitations. This is especially important since perception is the first level (level 1) of situational awareness. You cannot process and comprehend what you do not perceive.

perception

Vision: How you use your eyes to scan while driving can make a big difference in your ability to perceive and process enough of your environment to be safe. You have basically two types of vision; your central (focal) vision and your peripheral (ambient) vision. Your focal vision is very narrow, only approximately five degrees wide (depending on how it's defined), but allows you to see detail in the visual scene as well as judge distance accurately. Peripheral vision encompasses the remainder or majority of your vision – around your focal vision, not only side to side but above and below as well. Your peripheral vision is sensitive to light as well as motion, which probably kept your distant ancestors from being eaten by predators approaching them from the side. Vehicles and pedestrians entering your visual field from the side are detected by your peripheral vision. Once you are conscious of activity in your peripheral vision, you would direct your focal vision to pick up more detail, distance, and trend or closure information. This works well if you are interested in what's going on in your peripheral vision. If you are focused on a "side" task unrelated to driving – such as talking on a cell phone, or daydreaming, then you will more likely ignore those important peripheral cues. Our distant ancestors were really interested in not being eaten or killed. We seem to have become more complacent!

Imagine that you are the pilot flying an aircraft. While you scan out of the front windscreen, you can still detect an aircraft to the side that is moving relative to the horizon – left or right, forward or back, up or down. But what if there is an aircraft coming straight at you on a collision course? That aircraft would not be moving along the horizon – there would be no relative lateral or vertical motion. Even a large aircraft on a collision course within your peripheral field-of-view would merely look like a bug on the windscreen until it is literally within seconds of hitting you. Therefore, pilots must scan proactively forward and to the sides while flying.

In another scenario, let's say you are driving on a road in the countryside and you are approaching a cross road ahead. There is a vehicle on that cross road approaching the intersection at the same rate you are. There is a two-way stop sign at the intersection, and you have the right of way. Hopefully the driver of that other vehicle sees his stop sign because you may be unable to detect the vehicle in your peripheral vision until it is quite close. Why? Even though that vehicle is within your peripheral field of view, it is on a collision course with you, and there is no "line-of-sight (LOS)" movement in your visual scene. An object on a collision course with you presents no relative movement in your visual field and is difficult to detect in your peripheral vision. You would eventually detect it, but perhaps not until a collision is imminent, if you were visually or cognitively distracted, and were therefore either not visually scanning the environment, or not comprehending visual cues.

How to Scan: Fighter pilots use LOS rate at high speed passes to ensure they will not hit the other aircraft they are merging with. If the aircraft is moving left, right, up or down in the pilot's windscreen, then it is most probable that the two aircraft won't hit each other. Aviators know that the only reliable way to detect objects in their peripheral field that have low LOS rates is to actively scan by deliberately searching a section of the environment and then moving their central/focal vision deliberately to a neighboring section of the environment, deliberately focusing vision in each sector in turn. The segmented scanning technique is more effective than sweeping your eyes across the horizon when flying, since the latter technique may not allow you to pick up relatively small objects with low LOS rates but with potentially high closure rates. In the flying community, the largest transport category aircraft can appear "relatively small" in a pilot's field of view — like a fly speck on the windscreen — until it is close.

As a driver, your task of scanning is easier. A driver must typically only scan in azimuth (horizontally), on or at least near the horizon, versus scanning both in azimuth and in elevation (high and low), as pilots must do. And in the driving environment, where vehicles are moving much more slowly and potential closure rates of road vehicles are typically low compared to aircraft, sweeping your scan may not prove as disadvantageous as it typically is in the flying domain, where objects such as aircraft on a collision course are typically difficult to detect until collision is imminent. Nonetheless, while driving, focusing your central vision on an item of interest will allow you to better estimate distance and closure. This would be advantageous for instance, if you are planning to turn in front of opposing traffic. In this case, you could pause your scan to pick up detailed distance and closure information on the approaching traffic before turning. If you rush your scan, because you are impatient to turn, you may completely miss a harder to see vehicle; say one that is smaller, travelling faster and neutral in color. A scenario where you may be prone to this is anytime you must clear for traffic in both directions as you would when turning left across traffic into the far lanes. If you sweep your scan left and right too quickly across a wide azimuth, then you may miss critical traffic information.

An evolutionary aspect of human vision can help you detect detail of objects in your visual field while scanning. Your eyes naturally "fixate" for very brief periods of time with your focal vision naturally stopping to gather higher quality data on objects within the narrow central field of vision, before moving on. This causes what researchers describe as a jerky eye movement called "saccades." This is a good thing. Saccades allow your eyes to shift point of focus slightly on an item or items of interest in your visual scene to gather more detailed information on those items, and build a more detailed mental representation of your environment. Large head movements side-to-side with rapid sweeps may tend to override the advantage of these saccades. When you scan too rapidly, you may think you are gathering important data about potential threats, but you are probably overriding your vision's natural ability to gather important visual cues. You may see vehicles. But you may miss important details about them (turn signals, brake lights). And you may miss smaller elements in your environment completely, such as debris in the road, or an object about to hit your windshield. So, the next time you want to scan a wide azimuth (angular range across the horizon), stop to scan individual sectors, or at least scan as slowly and deliberately as is practical. Doing so will facilitate your vision's natural ability to gather more detailed information. If you are going to use a sweeping scan, then at least keep your scan rate (head and eye movement) reasonably slow or you will miss detailed information about objects in your visual field-of-view.

"Near Rocks Far Rocks:" When flying low and fast, tactical aviators have a saying—Near Rocks, Far Rocks—which reminds them of scanning priorities. "Near rocks, far rocks" indicates that pilots' attention should first be spent clearing terrain, towers, and other objects in their immediate path, or "near rocks"—clearing for what they must avoid and what could kill them the quickest; and then focusing on "far rocks," or on terrain and objects further in the distance for follow-on maneuvering decisions.

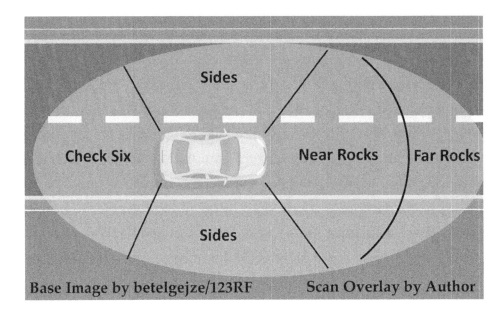

Base Image by betelgejze/123RF   Scan Overlay by Author

The same holds for drivers. You must first clear your near rocks or immediate path ahead (and in the direction of the turn if turning) so you can maintain proper spacing, and avoid hitting someone or something in your lane, or a vehicle moving into it. Many drivers erroneously scan low, looking down at the road in front of them. However, even when scanning for "near rocks" you should generally keep your scan high, at eye level parallel to the road surface. This is where most vehicles and other objects of interest will be. Very brief glances down at the road surface are OK, if necessary, to detect smaller objects or debris on the road surface, and to avoid them. After you've cleared your immediate path, you can then scan the "far rocks," shifting your attention further into the distance of your visual field. You can detect road conditions, slowing traffic, road signage, etc., that are not of immediate concern, but the awareness of which allows you to "plan your next move," so that you can drive more predictably and smoothly.

The pilot visual check mantra I learned as a new wingman in the F-16 was a little more complicated than "near rocks, far rocks." It was "near rocks, far rocks, lead, check six." When driving, we do not have a flight lead to clear through for threats, so let's make this **"near rocks, far rocks, sides, check six."** After checking near rocks, and then far rocks, briefly check "sides," or side to side using your focal vision to pick up more detail on objects and threats to the sides. This is especially important when crossing an intersection or in areas where there is heavy pedestrian traffic. Remember, when your traffic light turns green you may have the right-of-way, but another vehicle could run their red light and hit you.

My state, Arizona, is one of the top states for red light runners, and yes, I often see drivers run red lights, as well as enter an intersection to turn after the turn arrow has turned red. It is sad that these red-light runners feel entitled to do so—quite a hit on their character. Remember that point the next time you proceed into the intersection right as your light turns green only to be sideswiped by someone who just ran their light. You can be right and still end up dead if you do not practice defensive driving. Look out for pedestrians as well. When you are making a right turn onto a cross street at a red signal (in this example assuming you drive on the right side of the road), it is easy to neglect to clear right. After all, you are normally only worried about the traffic approaching from the left. But if you don't clear right you may miss a pedestrian or bicyclist about to cross, or, rarely, someone driving on the wrong side of the road; it's happened before (if a bicyclist is actually riding a bike, and not walking it, he or she should never ride opposite flow of traffic on or off sidewalk but it unfortunately occurs).

After checking sides, then "check six;" think clock positions where 12 o'clock is off the nose of your vehicle, 3 o'clock is to the right, 6 o'clock is behind you and 9 o'clock is to the left side. You check six by checking your rear-view and side mirrors, or by physically looking behind you, for instance, when clearing for traffic before changing lanes or to see who is approaching you from behind. Checking sides and six-o'clock will also help you pick up motorcyclists approaching from the rear and sides.

Scanning and Assessing: Most aviators have already learned the art of processing visual information that has left their visual field during scanning. An experienced and capable operator (driver, pilot, or any other vehicle or complex system operator) can briefly sample visual information, and then process that information while looking somewhere else. This is good, because staring at something to process and comprehend it takes up valuable time when you could be looking somewhere else. For instance, a driver can look in the rearview mirror, then, while moving his or her scan somewhere else, proceed to comprehend the information perceived in the rearview mirror (level 2 SA) and make decisions based on it (level 3 SA) while perceiving other information ahead. This ability, which can be learned by most individuals, can be bettered with practice. Not all people can form or retain a mental image of what they have just seen. For these individuals, visual information is lost when they divert their visual attention to something else. This does not mean that they should not drive, just that they must be extra careful. Of course, you cannot scan and assess effectively if you are cognitively distracted by mental tasks not pertinent to maintaining driving SA. But by now, you get that.

Limits to Visual Perception: Since driving is, for now, a very visually intensive task, our visual acuity and scanning skills are the core of safe driving, and are the basis for effective decision making. Aspects of our vision, such as binocular vision, afford us good depth perception and allow us to accurately judge distance. Many drivers lack good depth perception, but that limitation can be overcome to an extent. These drivers can learn to rely on line-of-sight (LOS) rates of objects, relative size of vehicles and other objects, and changes in the relative size those objects, based on experience and expectations. Excessive fatigue can cause temporary monocular vision, which is obviously dangerous in the driving environment if you are not expecting it to occur. Fatigue not only hampers your depth perception, but limits your SA at all levels (perception, comprehension, prediction, and decision making).

The contrast of objects in your visual field plays a critical role in discerning those objects against the background. The color of an object, ambient light level, and certain atmospheric conditions affect object contrast, or how well the object stands out against the background. Environmental conditions such as fog, haze and rain attenuate contrast, making everything in your visual field blend in, and reducing contrast of individual objects. Color plays a valuable role in detection of objects against certain backgrounds. What few studies performed on vehicle color vs. crash risk imply generally that silver, white and yellow cars are involved in less passive crashes (meaning, someone else hit you because they could not see you). Black cars seem to be involved in the most crashes—there is simply less color contrast of black cars in low light conditions and against a dark colored road surface. Of course, that black vehicle may be more visible than a white vehicle in blizzard conditions!

Your ability to discern color drops off dramatically when detection is shifted away from central vision and into your peripheral vision (it drops more dramatically in the red-green range than in the blue-yellow range). What colors are most visible depends on environmental conditions, and on the person viewing the scene. Many people have differing levels and types of color blindness.

Don't discount the value in vehicle lighting (either from daytime running lights, parking lights or headlights) in improving your visibility to other drivers despite the color of your vehicle. Having your lights on will also improve the ability of someone to see you in their peripheral vision; for instance, when they look back to clear behind them before changing lanes.

Speeding and Vision: The faster you drive, the more you are prone to the effects of tunnel vision. This occurs because objects in your peripheral vision begin to blur due to high line-of-sight rates. When this happens, your vision picks up less detail about these objects. To complicate matters, you have less time to make decisions because your speed relative to other objects increases. Also, as your absolute speed over the road increases, your distance travelled increases in the time it takes you to decide to do something and act, braking distance increases, and you are more prone to losing control of your vehicle.

hxdyl/123RF

Vehicle Blind Spots: Numerous blind spots exist due to the design of the vehicle you drive. Your window pillars (the vertical or near vertical pillars dividing the window area of a vehicle, labeled A, B, C, etc., from front to back), and even your rear-view mirror produce blind spots. Part of your scan should include physically moving your head to the side to see beyond those blind spots. The A-pillar blind spot (between the front windscreen and front side windows) could be large enough to preclude you from seeing a vehicle approaching from the forward side quadrant at an intersection in enough time to avoid it. Rear pillars can prevent you from seeing traffic behind you in an adjacent lane in your blind spot.

Corrective Lenses, Sunglasses and Driving: Just as blind spots exist with your vehicle, wearing eyeglasses or sunglasses inappropriate or less than optimum for driving can be problematic. The frames and arms of eye- and sun-glasses are built-in blind spots. Eyewear frames may be small, but when placed so close to your eyes, their "relative" size is very large, and they can block a significant portion of your total 360-degree field of view—so much so that they could completely mask a full-size vehicle in the not-so-far distance coming at you. In fact, they can block out more vision than the pillars of your vehicle. Having thick eyeglass arms can severely hamper your peripheral vision. If you wear "fashion-wear" eyeglasses or sunglasses with thick frames and arms (prescription or otherwise), it may be prudent for you to purchase a separate pair of driving glasses. Moving your head actively while scanning can prevent blind spots due to eye wear. You are probably not moving your head if you are zoning out or talking on a cell phone.

Mabel Amber/Pixabay

Another problem is that, if your vision has deteriorated to the point that you cannot physically discern objects beyond the boundary of your lenses, then, by wearing small-diameter prescription lenses while driving, you may be unnecessarily restricting your vision. Larger lenses are better for driving. Contacts can mitigate this problem. Also, when wearing sunglasses in bright conditions, the glare entering beyond the edges of your sunglass lenses may preclude your ability to see well. Wearing sunglasses with large lenses sufficiently wide can reduce this problem. The best driving eyewear would have relatively large lenses with anti-glare coating (this is good for nighttime driving as well), and with thin frames and arms. Also, the tint density should be as light as practical (transition or variable tint density lenses are generally not good for driving because you have no control over tint density; at any time the tint density could be either too light or too dark). Dark tinted sunglasses can easily block out as much as 40% or more of visible light, significantly hampering your ability to discern detail in the visual scene.

Choosing the right sunglass color tints is important. An informative article on Selectspecs.com ("How to Choose Safe Sunglasses for Driving") states that the best lens colors for driving are gray and brown, and the worst colors are pink, blue and green. Choosing the wrong color can adversely impact how well you can see road signs and traffic lights.

If you have color vision deficiency at any level, certain sunglass color tints may also significantly hamper your ability to adequately discern the color and contrast of traffic lights, and traffic signage. It is best to consult with your optometrist to decide what the best sunglass lens color for you would be while driving. In general, a true neutral gray lens color allows all colors to come through equally.

That may be a safe bet for all drivers. A research paper entitled "Sunglasses, Traffic Signals, and Color Deficiencies" (authors Dain S.J., Wood J.M., Atchison DA) from the FAAO School of Optometry and Vision Science, University of South Wales, Australia, can be a helpful source of information.

trendobjects/123RF

Empty Field Myopia: The eyes of a pilot who is visually scanning a clear blue sky with no clouds or other noticeable objects in the distance to focus on – an "empty visual field" - may begin to focus at a point very close to the aircraft, not off in the distance where they would be more apt to pick up approaching traffic. This is called empty field myopia and is of concern to pilots, especially when they are under Visual Flight Rules and must see and avoid other traffic, without positive air traffic control traffic separation.

On a clear day while driving, there are always enough objects in the distance to keep your eyes focused far enough ahead so that you can scan effectively. However, in conditions of low visibility such as rain,

fog, haze, smoke, or even nighttime, where objects i.
have lost a significant portion of their contrast, your ¿
focus at a distance very close to you, not further in
where you want them to focus. When driving, as your ___ucal
distance becomes near focused due to low contrast conditions, you
may miss a vehicle or object entering your visual field-of-view
ahead. Empty field myopia is not usually a problem in driving, but
it could be if visibility is very poor. And its effect could be
aggravated by having a contaminated windshield. Without anything
of contrast to focus on in the distance, your focus can be much more
easily drawn close by debris, bugs, and even raindrops on the
windshield. Moreover, when you daydream, zone out, or are
excessively fatigued, your eyes may not focus on anything even
when high contrast objects like cars and trees are available to focus
on in the distance.

Driving at Night: Driving at night poses its own unique challenges.
For one, the less light available, the darker objects are, and the less
detail there is. It is harder to see ahead and around you. If you are
familiar with your nighttime driving environment or have a low task
load, driving can seem more relaxing than driving during the
daytime. The reason for this is that your visual sensory system is less
saturated. There is simply less to see. The less you see, the less taxed
your brain is when processing this more limited information. The
challenge here is that none of those environmental elements— road
shoulders, obstacles, debris, unlighted vehicles—that were there
during the daytime went away at night. They are all still there posing
as potential hazards. What we do not see can hurt us. For this reason,
we simply must be more careful and diligent at night. To complicate

tters, most of us are generally more fatigued at night after a long day—and this adversely affects our visual scan and SA. To understand how dangerous nighttime driving can be, consider that the National Highway Traffic Administration states that over half of driving fatalities occur at night even though only about a quarter of driving typically takes place then.

route55/123RF

At night, you see less detail in your central or focal vision. The darker it is, the less color there is. One could argue that color does not exist when it is completely dark; only the potential for color exists. For instance, a red car a has chemical pigment in its paint to reflect red light, but when there is very little light hitting it, your eyes may no longer detect that it is red. Because colors are not as obvious at night, color contrast lessens dramatically. Depth perception and peripheral vision are also hampered at night.

At night, your central or focal vision does not work very well at all. Your focal vision may still be adequately effective in a brightly lit city driving scene. However, as you progress to dimly lit rural driving environments, your focal vision loses effectiveness. There are two types of photoreceptors in the retina of your eyes that contribute directly to your sight – cones and rods. The cones, that are used for focal vision, need significant light levels to be effective and can discriminate colors very well. They lose effectiveness in low light conditions. Rods, located outside the central part of the retina, are very effective at extremely low light levels but cannot discriminate color. If it is dark enough out, staring at a small object in the distance that lies completely within your narrow focal field-of-view, where your cone photoreceptors are active, could cause that object to remain unseen in your visual field.

Star gazers that wish to see dim celestial objects in the night sky, and pilots that must see dimly lit objects in the distance on the ground, use the technique of "averted vision" to see those objects. Averted vision is shifting your focus into your peripheral vision slightly and exploiting the lower light detection capability of the rods in your eyes. Doing so can allow you to see small dimly lit objects at night. Chances are, in routine driving environments, you will never have to use this technique. And pausing your scan too long in any fashion when driving during the day or night can be dangerous anyway. Nonetheless, scanning slowly and deliberately at night can maximize your ability to see obstacles in the distance, and can exploit the advantages of both cone and rod photoreceptors.

At night, on dimly lit roads, you can only see as far as your headlights. If you detect an obstacle in the road and must stop suddenly, your vehicle's stopping distance may exceed your headlight illumination distance, even at legal road speeds. Pedestrians who cross in front may appear out of nowhere since they were outside of your headlight beam until they cross (about 75% of pedestrians killed by vehicles at night crossed roads at other than designated crosswalks). Therefore, under very low light conditions, it may be prudent to drive more slowly. Vehicle headlights may become misaligned after an accident, when changed, or over time. You can usually easily manually adjust or aim your vehicle's headlights for optimum lateral and vertical alignment (your vehicle's operating manual may give guidance on how to do so).

If you must use your high beams to see further ahead at night, turn them to back to low beam before other vehicles enter their beam. They can be a hazard to other drivers. Bright lights constrict your pupils and prevent light from other more dimly lit objects in your field of view from reaching your eyes. It is a good idea to avoid staring directly at bright lights while you drive. It can take up to 30 minutes for your eyes to become optimally sensitive to light again after viewing a bright light. Ideally, you should avoid bright lights within 30 minutes of driving in poorly illuminated areas, but that is not usually practical. Fortunately, most of your night vision comes back within about five minutes of encountering a bright light. If you are temporarily night "blinded," immediately focus your attention to your lane boundary lines while attempting to scan far enough ahead to avoid vehicles and obstacles in your path, and slow down if required, while being predictable to other drivers.

Before you even drive, set up your interior lights properly. It is tempting to turn up your instrument displays bright at night, but this is exactly what you do not want to do. Having bright interior lights effectively reduces your visual acuity outside of the vehicle. Again, these bright lights inside your vehicle constrict your pupils, restricting your vision outside your vehicle. You want to have all interior lights turned down as low as practical and still see the indications adequately. Aviators know this.

Before you drive at night it would be wise to prepare yourself and to set your vehicle up properly. If you wear corrective lenses during the day, then it is especially important to wear them at night. There is a lot of hype going around about tinted eyewear that enhances night vision. Yellow tinted lenses, for instance, have been touted as making you better able to see at night. They may help you see better in foggy or hazy daylight conditions by improving contrast. The problem with applying any color tint or shade to lenses is that it will measurably decrease the amount of light that reaches your eyes. And that will decrease detail of objects even further at night. Anti-glare coatings can aid vision at night, but they can be obtained in clear lenses. We have discussed vision but your other senses can play an important role in situational awareness when driving.

Hearing: Hearing can be a valuable aid to maintaining situational awareness when driving. It is not a bad idea to keep an ear free to listen for the sirens of emergency responders. In fact, it is generally illegal to wear ear buds in both ears while driving, riding, or bicycling on public roads. Before backing your vehicle up, it is, as a technique, a good idea to turn your radio off, and you're A/C down or off if noisy as precautions to enable you to hear something or someone behind you that you may have missed. Backing up slowly will make you predictable, allowing people and vehicles you don't see enough time to get out of the way or warn you of their presence. If you are in a safe location to do so, walk behind your vehicle before getting in to check for children or pets, and roll your windows down, even partially, to be able to hear noises outside the vehicle.

Listening can be a good way also of detecting problems developing with your vehicle. A squealing sound can mean that your brake pads are nearing the end of their useful life. In fact brakes have a built-in wear indicator that will cause this squeal, which may be intermittent at first. If you hear clicking in the front of your vehicle and notice that steering feels loose, then you may have worn tie rod ends or lower ball joints. These problems can become serious. A mechanical knocking, clicking or popping sound when turning can mean that one of your CV (constant velocity) joints is bad. If a CV joint fails, it can render your vehicle un-drivable.

Kinesthetic Sense: Your kinesthetic sense and somatosensory system are important for detecting vibrations that might be indicative of a maintenance problem with your vehicle. You might detect them in your "seat-of-the-pants"—a vibration through the seat, or through the steering wheel itself. Vibrations in the steering wheel can be indicative of a serious problem developing.

Smell: Smell and its companion sense of taste can alert you to fuel leaks, smoldering wires, or a fire developing.

Your Sixth Sense: The sixth sense or extra sense is usually defined as your intuitive or perceptive power. In a strictly spiritual sense, if it exists at all, this sense is probably not something most of us could ever tap into. However, when defined more in practical terms of intuition or perceptive power, it is real and can come in handy. What are some examples of your sixth sense at work? One is when you sense impending danger. Perhaps it is a feeling that you should slow down, or look in a certain direction, or just pull over.

Bruce Rolff/123RF

What you may not realize are the real physiological and explainable reasons for this sixth sense. Your senses—vision, hearing, feel, smell—are constantly assimilating an enormous amount of data that is input into your brain. Your peripheral vision, while not sensitive to color or detail, can detect very subtle motion cues. You cannot be keenly consciously aware of all or even most of this data entering your brain. While you are paying attention to obvious sensory cues, there may be data that your brain is assessing that you are not aware of. Your brain is continuously involved in what is called pre-attentive subconscious processing. This is the subconscious accumulation of data from the environment. Your brain will pick out the most salient data to pay the most attention to. But some of that subconscious data that you are not overtly aware of may trigger a sixth sense feeling. Maybe you were aware for a fraction of a second of a sensory cue, but then it was replaced in your conscious memory by other cues. Some of that data is lurking in your memory and hinting that you should do something with it.

For instance, your situational awareness tells you that no one is behind you and to your right while driving on the road. You are certain that you cleared the lane and decide to change lanes. But something tells you to look one more time. You do, and luckily so, because there is a vehicle approaching fast in that lane. Had you relied on your conscious SA as it existed before that one last look, you would have caused a collision. Perhaps your sixth sense tells you to duck, but you have no conscious clue why. You do anyway, just before a large rock slams through the windshield. Your brain probably tapped into a peripheral visual cue of the rock being slung by a truck while you were consciously attentive to other cues.

Maybe your sixth sense gives you a general uneasy feeling; one that says, get off the road. You do not know why, but you do, only to avoid a multi vehicle pile-up seconds or even moments later. Your experience may come into play here in very subtle ways. For instance, although there are no distinct markers signifying an immediate need to pull over, your overall sensory input combined with experience tells you that something is not the way it should be. Other drivers are behaving in an unusual manner. The weather conditions are abnormal; road conditions are not the same as they usually are. You do not feel right about it. Pilots are usually good about using their sixth sense. For instance, when flying, we travel through potentially adverse weather all the time. When the weather is strange, and it does not fit our expectations based on the past, we react to it perhaps by seeking better conditions immediately. Why? Our lives depend on it.

You may be driving down the interstate and notice unusually gusty winds from the side, and may not consciously recollect that the large semi-truck with trailer that you are about to pass has a tremendous amount of side surface area, which when subject to those winds, causes that truck to have a much higher propensity to topple over. You may, however, have a "feeling"—a distant memory from your collective life experience in your conscience—enough to give you the feeling that you should not pass that truck. Something tells you that it is not a good idea. If this feeling is based on your intuition and you are not sure where it came from, then it is your sixth sense. One thing for sure is, if you make a habit of being a distracted driver, your sixth sense will be poor at best.

Factors Effecting Sensory Perception and Comprehension: Your experience as a driver can affect your ability to achieve a high level of situational awareness.

Complacency: Experience is generally a good thing. But complacency is an experience trap that should be avoided. Whereas a novice driver may have senses attuned to just about anything that comes his or her way, an experienced driver can, over time, come to be detuned to various road hazards, or may fall into the habit of just not taking them seriously since statistically they may never have been a problem in the past. For instance, a driver may become complacent in turning aggressively into traffic in familiar road conditions because it has always worked in the past. That driver may not be aware of how close he or she is to losing traction and skidding out—until it happens. Other examples of complacency are not clearing properly before changing lanes, not looking both ways before crossing intersections, not initially turning into the closest lane or assigned lane, etc. And of course, there is being distracted by texting, talking on a cell phone, etc.

SA Field Saturation and High Task Workload: SA field saturation and conditions of high driver task workload can hamper SA as well. SA field saturation occurs when the amount of data that the brain is attempting to consciously process becomes overwhelming, causing other important sensory cues not to be processed. This may happen because there is just so much going on in the immediate driving environment. It could be that the driver is already cognitively distracted by other mental tasks such as being anxious about a non-driving event (perhaps related to work, relationship, health, finances, etc.), or that the driver is attempting to pay too much attention to things that do not matter, leaving less cognitive room for things that do matter. This happens more often with less experienced drivers.

Confirmation Bias: Another factor affecting perception and comprehension of important environmental cues is confirmation bias, which is a type of cognitive bias. Confirmation bias is the tendency to not only recall, but also favor and seek out environmental cues in a way that confirms one's preexisting beliefs or expectations. As discussed before, you can have high situational awareness on certain elements of your driving environment…and low or no SA on other elements. You cannot have high SA on all elements in your driving environment – there is too much going on around you for your brain to process; but you need enough SA on enough elements in your driving domain to allow you to make the right decisions to stay alive. Confirmation bias causes you to perceive selective information (skewed level 1 SA) and to miss other information. And it also causes you to process or comprehend information based on your expectations (skewed lev el 2 SA). Many drivers think they are better than they are. After all, you may think, "only other drivers that get into accidents." If you think you are better than that, you will think that it is OK for you to drive distracted (e.g. texting), aggressively (e.g. fast or recklessly), or complacently (e.g. always veering across lanes in a turn, or not using turn signals properly). Unfortunately, sometimes it takes a close call or accident to cure of us of this bias (assuming we survive to learn our lesson). Confirmation bias can cause a driver to "act in the wrong scene."

Acting in the Wrong Scene: Remember that your mental model of the driving environment or domain, indeed any domain, does not represent the actual environment fully, and can at times be downright inadequate or wrong. Examples of confirmation bias causing a driver to act in the wrong scene may include expectations that, when turning right onto a crossroad, there will never be a bicyclist or pedestrian about to cross the immediate lane or crosswalk from the right side against traffic. For me personally, there are certain intersections in my community, where I habitually clear right before turning right. Then there are certain intersections such as those just after a highway off-ramp, where I must remind myself to clear right because I have expectations that no pedestrian or bicyclist would ever cross that intersection from the right. And how many of us expect a wrong way driver?

Another example of confirmation bias is a driver's expectation, mentioned earlier, that there will be no vehicles in low-light conditions without headlights on. Therefore, that driver only seeks out headlights to determine when to make a turn clear of traffic. The driver ignores cues of a vehicle approaching without lights on, even if the brain may have subconsciously detected those cues. The assumption or bias that you are safe to cross an intersection on a green light (or two- or four-way stop sign) without clearing left and right can result in you getting T-boned at an intersection, which is very deadly (this killed an Air Force T-37 instructor at Williams Air Force Base right before my class started pilot training in 1987—a sad welcome for sure). Since your bias is that drivers won't run red lights or stop signs, at least not in your driving domain, you don't even engage in level 1 SA to scan and perceive a vehicle about to do so. Confirmation bias, or false expectations, lead to faulty perception of the environment and faulty decision making.

CHAPTER SEVEN: DRIVER DECISION MAKING

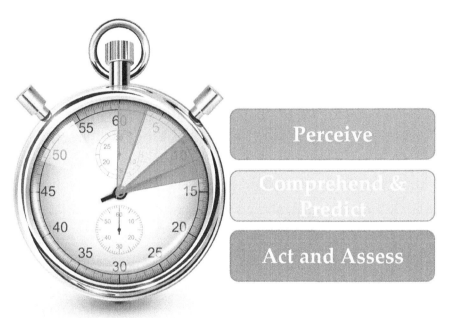

Stopwatch Vector by cobalt/123RF   SA Overlay by Author

Focused Situation Assessment Based on Priorities: The key to maintaining high situational awareness is focused situation assessment based on priorities, while avoiding complacency and confirmation bias. The best way to do this is to expect the unexpected, and to realize that you are just as vulnerable to an accident as any other driver. You must scan inside and outside your comfort zone. The dynamic nature of traffic requires constant effort to keep SA high. Focus your attention on safety related tasks first.

Primary attention should usually be devoted to the road ahead. Focus on near rocks, then far rocks, then sides and then behind you. Allocate attention based on your task. For instance, the frequency with which you check 6 by looking to the rear of the vehicle depends on whether you plan to remain in your lane or engage in a lane change. If you are not planning a lane change, the frequency with which you check 6 may lessen, but periodic scanning behind you is still important for contingency or crisis planning; for instance, knowing who is around you if you must maneuver suddenly. It is important to do repetitive sampling of the most important elements or threats, such as potential cross traffic at intersections, and erratic drivers. After safety-related cues are tended to, you can then bias attention towards your other objectives, such as navigation. The process is then repeated, always going back to priority safety-related tasks.

Driving Decision Making: At the end of the day, the reason we engage in situational awareness is to make effective decisions. In the flying world, this is called Aeronautical Decision Making (ADM). So perhaps we can call it Operator Decision Making (ODM), or more specifically, Driver Decision Making or DDM here. SA is the basis for sound decision making. Of course, just because you have high SA does not mean that you will act smartly.

Potential Crisis Awareness and a Maneuvering Mental Model: Sound DDM is important as are sound driving and maneuvering skills. It is also important, as part of maintaining high SA, to engage in potential crisis awareness. Then, you will not be startled or non-reactive due to panic should a bad situation occur. Potential crisis awareness—or what can get you into trouble during each phase of your driving activity—improves with your driver experience. You should ask yourself, for instance, when you back out of your driveway, turn left out of your residential area into traffic, merge onto the highway, etc., "What can go wrong here?" "What am I missing here?" Part of your SA mental model should be a "maneuvering mental model"—or how you would maneuver in a crisis if it happened right now. This is especially worthwhile given that many accidents occur due to driver over-controlling due to startle and not being prepared. As said earlier, it would not be a bad idea for you to seek out skill development in defensive maneuvering by taking a defensive driving course.

Task Prioritization—Avoiding Mental or Cognitive Overload: To avoid cognitive task saturation, it is important to prioritize tasks. This is one of the first things pilots learn, certainly military pilots, from my experience. When you become "task saturated," a term we use in the United States Air Force to describe a condition where the pilot reaches a level where he or she is dangerously overloaded with information - your attention capture is degraded. This means that your ability to focus your attention on something is inhibited. In fact, all levels of SA are inhibited. Short term memory processing lessens, you get tunnel vision and even your focal vision is degraded. Decision making is compromised. Reaction time becomes longer.

One of the best ways to avoid cognitive overload is to practice attention allocation. Know where to focus your attention based on your safety first, and then on your other priorities or goals (we just discussed this in the Focused Situation Assessment section). Fixating on your GPS display, or maneuvering hastily without proper SA to do so because your navigation system told you that you must do a legal U-Turn may be important to you. It is, however, not as

Ioulia Bolchakova/123RF

important as avoiding an accident as you juggle yourself in rush hour traffic. If things are so hectic on the road that all you can do is stay in your lane and avoid other traffic, then do that until you can safely work yourself out of the situation.

Yes, non-safety related tasks that you must temporarily place on hold will eventually become more important; navigation tasks can be resumed when you are less task saturated. Fuel will start to become a priority as you run low on fuel. My point is that all essential driving tasks will eventually become a priority. Your job is to pare away the barrage of potential sensory and cognitive inputs and focus on tasks in descending order of priority.

If things are just too busy for you, there are some things that you can do. Remain predictable in traffic and do not maneuver abruptly. Slow down while remaining safe. The dynamic nature of your environment settles down if you slow down. If that does not work, then remove yourself from the threat. Find the nearest exit or pull off into a parking lot and give yourself a chance to gather your wits.

Consider each of your driving tasks as a different fluid flowing into a bucket. There is a drain at the bottom of the bucket representing your processing time. When you are not task overloaded, the amount of data (fluid) flowing into the bucket is always less than or equal to or the amount flowing out. When you are task-saturated, the bucket fills up and eventually overflows. Your job is to make sure that what overflows – what does not get processed by your brain - is not what is needed to keep you alive. For that reason, what goes into the bucket first is the "fluid" or data representing your attention to the tasks that will keep you alive.

These tasks include active scanning to know what is going on immediately around you—location of other vehicles, obstacles, road surface, traffic behavior up ahead, etc. Navigation is not as important as spatial and traffic awareness. You can catch up with navigation when you have safety related tasks under control. By planning well in advance and always having plenty of fuel reserves, you can avoid fuel becoming a top priority at an inopportune time. Even the maintenance status of your car can become a top priority if you neglect it long enough; and then your tire blows out or your brakes or steering fail. Take care of your vehicle with preventative maintenance so that it never becomes a safety priority.

Leaving Yourself and the Other Driver an Out: When driving, it is a good idea to leave yourself an "out." This means always having some place to go to avoid an accident. You can only do this if you engage in high situational awareness all the time and know who is around you always, where the nearest exit is, what road hazards exist, and where you would not want to go if you had to pull over. For instance, you should always know where there is a safe, adequate shoulder, and where there is not. Similarly, it is also beneficial to always leave an out for the vehicles, including motorcycles, that you do not see. No one has perfect SA all the time. You may be completely unaware of a vehicle in the lane you are turning or merging into. Always leaving yourself and the other driver an out is absolutely the most violated common-sense driving rule I have ever seen, and it can get you into an accident.

Here is a scenario: You have just exited the highway eastbound and have come to a stop at the red light. You are in the right lane with your turn signal on. You look left to clear the southbound lanes that you are about to turn right onto. You are even diligent enough to clear right to ensure no pedestrians or bicyclists were about to cross from the right, in front of you. You do not see any vehicles in any of the three southbound lanes of traffic about to enter the intersection. You decide to turn, not into the rightmost lane - which is the safest, and in many locations, the only legal option assuming there is only one turn lane – but instead, cross into the middle lane. You thought about going all the way to the left lane because of your upcoming left turn, but today you did not. And that was a good thing, because, just as you turn into the middle lane, a driver swoops by you in the leftmost lane. You did not see that vehicle because it was dawn and the driver did not have his headlights on. Had you turned right and crossed all lanes you would have collided with that vehicle. This happened to me a year or so ago. I was fortunate. I realized afterward that it was not wise for me to cross into the middle lane. I should have initially turned into the right lane and then cleared each lane, while signaling my intentions in advance, before changing into the middle and then left lane. I was lucky—I could have crossed into the leftmost lane. If you think about it, by doing so, you would give the driver of a vehicle that you did not see an "out." Of course, if there is more than one turn lane, then you should turn into your assigned lane.

Even if you had missed a vehicle approaching the intersection in the rightmost lane, by turning initially into that lane, you maximize the opportunity of an unseen driver to avoid you, which he could do by maneuvering into an adjacent lane. You have also remained predictable, increasing the likelihood of other drivers avoiding an accident. In some states in the U.S., you are not legally bound to turning into the closest lane. The same is true for left turns, although left turns must always yield to opposing traffic. Still, by always turning into the closest lane whether right or left turn, and then signaling your intentions before changing into adjacent lanes, you give yourself and any unseen traffic an out. Just because it is legal to do something does not necessarily mean it is the most conservative option.

CHAPTER EIGHT: LIST OF DO'S AND DON'TS

ileezhun/123RF

The following is a summary of essential "do's and don'ts" when driving, to stay alive:

1. Learn and practice high situational awareness (Chapters 4-7). Learning and practicing the principles of situational awareness found in this guide will help you be more aware on the road, make better decisions, and hopefully avoid a crash. These principles can be applied to activities that you engage in other than driving (boating, flying, off-roading, running in the park, walking to your car at night, etc.).

2. Have high situational awareness (SA) before you need it (Chapter 4). Once you need it, it's too late in many cases. And distraction will ensure you don't have it. In aviation, the phrase "stay ahead of your aircraft" means that you should keep your SA high, plan effectively and keep up with critical mission and safety tasks. Otherwise, you'll get behind in critical tasks and feel like you are "hanging onto the wing." Likewise, when driving, you want to stay ahead and keep your SA high at all times.

3. Don't think that you are great at multitasking (Chapter 4). Multitasking is a myth. You cannot perform two complex tasks well simultaneously. For instance, your awareness of what is going on around can diminish significantly while holding a conversation with a passenger or on a cell phone.

4. Drive responsibly and understand the lethality of your vehicle (Chapter 2). If you drive distracted, which means with low SA, then you are using your vehicle as a potentially lethal weapon. If you cause a fatality, you can be charged with unintentional vehicular manslaughter.

5. Set up your vehicle before you drive, to include mirror and seat— be "one with your vehicle (Chapter 5)." Any good aviator knows to strap in securely, and to have access to all controls at all times. Likewise, as a driver, you should be "one" with your vehicle. Setting up your seat position and mirrors, to maximize your visual field-of-view forward, to the sides and to the rear, and buckling in, will increase your ability to maintain high SA, and survive a crash as well. Adjust your interior lights at night so that they are only bright

enough to clearly read important information; dimmer is better. Also, wear appropriate eyewear for daytime and night time driving.

6. Minimize distraction (visual, cognitive, manual). Never text and drive. Never engage in distractions like gaming while driving (Chapter 3). Texting or gaming while driving involves all three forms of distraction. If you engage in these activities while driving, you are a severe hazard on the road. But even talking on a cell phone can lower your SA enough to cause a crash. And just because you have technology that displays infotainment on a pop-up, or heads-up display, does not mean it is not a potentially fatal distraction.

7. Keep your vehicle maintained (brakes, tires) (Chapter 5). It is illegal to drive a poorly maintained vehicle. Doing so can cause a crash you otherwise could have avoided. Preventative maintenance is your obligation, not discretion, when you use public roads.

8. Plan your trip before you get in your vehicle (Chapter 5). Regardless of technology available in modern vehicles, looking at a GPS display or even listening to navigation voice commands is a distraction. You should at least be familiar with your route before you embark on your trip. The less you must look at a navigation display or rely on voice commands to get you where you are going, the better.

9. Choose a driving environment that is not too challenging considering your limitations and your vehicle's limitations (Chapter 2). Always assess yourself, your vehicle, and your environment. If

the odds are stacking up against you, choose a more conservative driving environment (e.g. back roads vs. highway) that fits your current limitations (e.g. fatigue, experience), your vehicle's limitations (e.g. soft brakes, low tire tread), or environmental hazards (e.g. rain slick roads).

10. Do not drive under the influence, while intoxicated (Chapter 3), or while overly fatigued (Chapter 5). DUI or DWI implies that you are incapable of operating a motor vehicle safely in the judgement of law enforcement. Alcohol, illegal drugs, legal marijuana, prescription and over-the-counter drugs can all render you sufficiently impaired to be charged with DUI or DWI. Driving overly fatigued has the same effect as DUI, and you can be held liable if you cause a crash. You owe it to those around you to be responsible and to not put lives unnecessarily at risk.

11. Know your personality limitations (e.g. are you impulsive, prone to rage, resigned, invulnerable?) (Chapter 5). Understanding your personality or behavior limitations can help you overcome them on the road and be a safer, more compassionate driver. If you are an aggressive driver, or if you have a propensity to punish other drivers for their mistakes, you are a menace. Take an anger management class or get off the road. You make mistakes as well. Learn to forgive. Remember, your vehicle has a tremendous capacity to kill people. You can be charged with vehicular homicide if your road rage kills someone. Understand also, that being overly conservative can cause a crash. And resignation in the face of crisis can prevent the take charge attitude that can help you survive.

12. Always make the goal of safety a priority over getting somewhere (Chapter 5). If you feel you must make your exit or cross all lanes in heavy traffic to make your turn—no matter what—then you are setting yourself up for an accident. If you see your exit at the last second and veer across the exit gore, then you are driving illegally and may hit someone you did not see. Decide right now never to act impulsively. Act instead smoothly and predictably, taking a later exit, for instance, if necessary. It's better to miss your exit or turn then to act impulsively and kill someone.

13. Always ask yourself, "what could go wrong here"—"What-If:" Ask yourself, what could go wrong in your current environment— and what would you do? Where would you go (Chapters 5, 7)? The moment you must maneuver to avoid something, or the moment that you have a tire blowout, failed brakes, or engine problem, is not the time to determine who is around you. You must already be aware of other vehicles around you and where you would maneuver when a crisis happens, to be truly safe.

14. Avoid overreacting and over-controlling in a crisis due to startle and low SA (Chapter 5). Over controlling your vehicle can cause a rollover, or cause you to hit another vehicle, both of which could be deadly. By being ready for anything, and avoiding surprise, startle or panic, you increase your chances of maintaining control in a crisis.

15. Signal your intentions in advance (Chapter 5): By using your turn signals to signal your intentions early, you can vastly increase your chances of avoiding an accident. A turn signal can also help that

driver or motorcyclist you did not see avoid you as you cross lanes. If you change lanes without signaling, and proceed to hit someone, you are in serious error and potentially liable. Signaling can not only help other drivers accommodate you, it can also alert the driver or operator you do not see have a chance to avoid you as you maneuver into them (see "Give the other Driver an Out," below). Even tapping your brakes to signal you will be braking can warn a driver tailgating you to back off (but "brake checking" is not smart). Nothing "signals" a poor or lazy driver more than one who does not signal well in advance.

16. Be a good wingman (Chapter 5). Although the concept of being a good wingman has its origins in tactical aviation, you can be a good wingman to others on the road just by being compassionate, courteous and predictable.

17. But never place blind faith in other drivers (Chapter 5). Most likely, you don't know the drivers on the road around you. They may prove to be predictable and courteous, but you never know what their skill level is, how they will react to a situation, or whether or not they even see you. How you react to unpredictable drivers is a "no brainer." You should consider them as a threat. Maintain SA on them and avoid them. But be wary of all drivers, even the ones that seem trustworthy. Do not tailgate, don't stay in someone's blind spot, and when possible, don't drive beside other vehicles, just in case they must maneuver. Of course, in heavy traffic, you may not be able to avoid blind spots or remaining next to other vehicles at normal road or highway speeds. But when you tailgate, you are putting blind faith not only in the driver ahead of you, but also in

drivers ahead of that driver. If the driver ahead of you brakes suddenly, you may be unable to avoid a rear end collision.

18. Clear the rear of your vehicle before you back up (Chapter 6). Backing up out of a driveway or parking space is hazardous. Visually clearing the back of your vehicle as you approach it (before you get in), if it is safe to do so, may allow you to see a child, pet or obstacle that may otherwise remain unseen once you are in the vehicle. Since your rearward vision is limited once you are in your vehicle, minimizing distraction by keeping air conditioning or heat, as well as music on low or off as you back up, can help you listen for cues that there is a potential conflict (child or approaching vehicle). Rolling down your windows before backing up—if it is safe to so— can help you hear sounds that may indicate that someone or something is behind you or approaching from a blind spot. Before you back up, ensure your mirrors are set up properly. Back up slowly and be predictable.

19. Don't speed (Chapter 6). Speeding lowers your SA and visual scanning ability, increases reaction time and stopping distance, makes you less predictable, increases your control loss potential, and exponentially increases the lethality of a crash.

20. Always give yourself "an out." (Chapter 7). By always practicing and having high SA, you always know what is around you, and where you would go if you had to maneuver in a crisis. Know if the lane to your left and right is clear. Know the condition of the left and right shoulders. Be prepared.

21. Give the driver you do not see "an out." (Chapter 7). Drive as though there are other unseen drivers in your vicinity, and maneuver in a predictable and smooth manner so that they can avoid you if necessary. Signaling is one way to do this. Another way is to turn into the nearest lane, giving a driver you don't see the adjacent lanes to avoid you. If you turn or veer across lanes, you are unpredictable to other drivers. If you cut in front of a driver you don't see, you don't give that driver a chance to avoid you.

22. Practice defensive driving (Chapter 5). You can drive completely within legal bounds and still be involved in a crash you could have avoided by simply practicing defensive driving. Practicing high SA and being ready to react to a crisis is the essence of defensive driving. You can remain in your lane, at the speed limit, but blissfully unaware of what is going on around you. If someone hits you due to their error, you can still be injured in a crash that you could have avoided.

23. Learn effective visual scanning (Chapter 6). Learn about central and peripheral vision and limitations, how to scan near, far, sides and rear. Learn how to scan to see smaller vehicles or vehicles on a collision course. Learn the limitations of night vision.

24. Drive under the premise that traffic is a living breathing entity; you are either contributing to safe driving or you are part of the problem (Chapter 5, Conclusion). Ask yourself, "am I helping the efficient flow of traffic, or am I being selfish." You can help by being smooth and predictable. You generally hurt the efficient flow of traffic by being unpredictable, too fast or too slow, erratic, maintaining too much spacing in slow traffic or in jams, not being at

highway speed when merging, etc.). Driving is a balance. You always want to be predictable which means not driving aggressively or erratically. However, being over-conservative may get you into trouble, and cause trouble for other drivers.

CHAPTER NINE: AUTOMOBILE
TECHNOLOGY TODAY AND FUTURE

cheskyw/123RF

D on Sherman of Car and Driver Magazine said it best: "Sadly, we are a nation of mediocre drivers, distracted on our daily journeys by dining, child rearing, makeup applying, and incessant texting. Driver's Ed is a shadow of its former self, and few of us can use the accident-avoidance capabilities built into every new car. Our driving errors cause crashes, injuries, and fatalities. So, while we're getting worse behind the wheel, the sensors and algorithms capable of saving us from ourselves are getting better."

It is important, when shopping for a vehicle, to know what technology you want, and to ask the right questions. Consider these factors though: complexity of vehicle systems that warrant or need our cognitive attention can be a harmful distraction if not used properly. The ever-increasing availability and complexity of navigation, infotainment and other driver attention-intensive technology seems to have, in the short term, outpaced safety systems that can compensate for that distraction. Safety systems that can "save us from ourselves" are rapidly improving. But, for now, it is up to you to avoid lethal distraction. The right technology used at the wrong time or in the wrong way can cause an accident. And active systems that are designed to avoid a crash cannot be used as a crutch. Also, you must understand the capabilities and limitations of such systems. The following are some technologies that can enhance safety.

Airbags: Airbags are an essential part of any vehicle purchase. There are several different types of airbags, the most prevalent being frontal driver and passenger airbags, side curtain airbags and side torso airbags. There are also rear curtain, knee, seat cushion, center and seatbelt airbags, although this list is not all inclusive. These systems are designed as Supplemental Restraint Systems (SRS). This means that they are meant to supplement the use of seat belts and shoulder harnesses, not to replace them. In fact, not using seat belts can negate the advantages of airbags. It is important to adhere to guidance and warnings with airbags, especially since they can injure or kill small children or infants. Also, if an airbag deploys, you want to be at the proper distance from it and at the proper position. Consider the explosive force of an airbag and how it deploys. You could sustain serious injury if, at the time of airbag deployment, you are not wearing your safety belts, are leaning forward, have your hands high on the steering wheel, arms crossed, hand on the horn, have your feet up on the dash, are leaning against a window, or have objects between you and the airbag. Sit a safe distance away from the front airbag and do not tilt the steering wheel excessively high. Given current recalls on airbags, the automobile safety industry has a long way to go to develop significantly better airbags that save lives in severe accidents, without unnecessarily injuring vehicle occupants, for instance, in relatively minor fender benders.

Tire Pressure Monitoring System (TPMS): Many modern vehicles have TPMS. Many drivers rely on this system to tell them when to inflate their tires. Unfortunately, this is not a smart idea. Often, TPMS will only warn you when your tires are 25% below recommended inflation pressure. At this point, you are already in danger of having an early tire failure and excessive tire damage may already be occurring. TPMS is only meant as a final warning that your tire pressure is way too low. It does not replace regular monitoring. You would be wise to buy a reliable tire pressure gage. I personally like dial or digital gages over stick gages, but not all are created equal. Tire gages are most accurate at room temperature.

Telematics: General Motor's OnStar system introduced in 1995 is an example of vehicle telematics. It is usually a subscription service. A vehicle's telematics system receives wireless and cellular signals (and can connect with your phone in some cases) and processes information to do a variety of useful things. It can route you around accidents, provide remote key access (if you lock your keys in your car), summon roadside assistance, and can increasingly provide satellite weather, and infotainment. One great feature of telematics is automatic crash notification (ACN). If you are involved in an accident significant enough to trigger ACN, your vehicle telematics will automatically summon emergency services.

Anti-Lock Braking Systems (ABS): Modern ABS not only prevents wheel lock up and skidding during braking but modern systems also control front and rear braking distribution.

Traction Control: Whereas ABS prevents wheel lock up during braking, Traction Control prevents loss of traction during acceleration. Traction control does not help with steering as Electronic Stability Control does (see below).

Electronic Stability Systems (ECS): ECS should be considered an essential feature of a new car purchase if you are serious about safety and you are not a seasoned race car driver. The Insurance Institute for Highway Safety and the U.S. National Highway Traffic Safety Administration state that one-third of fatal accidents could be prevented by the use of this technology. ECS takes ABS to a whole new level. This system uses automatic differential wheel braking and engine deceleration, as required, to help you maintain traction while steering or maneuvering. It compares what the driver wants to do (by measuring steering input) with the vehicle path. For instance, when a driver makes a steering input to avoid a collision, the vehicle under steers typically (it lags the steering input). ECS applies braking to the rear wheel inside the turn to get the vehicle going immediately where the driver wants. When the driver corrects back, the vehicle may tend to over steer or begin skidding. ECS then applies braking to the front wheel outside of the turn to bring the vehicle back in line with intended steering.

ECS can also manipulate engine power and transmission to aid traction. ECS will notify the driver when it has intervened, so that the driver does not become overconfident or complacent, believing he or she is maneuvering well within the capabilities of the vehicle. There are many different manufacturer names for ECS, so ask if an advertised system is ECS and what its capabilities are.

Rearview Back-Up Camera and Back-Up Radar Warning: Rearview back-up cameras, which can be easily added aftermarket, help drivers see what is behind them. A rear- back-up radar warning system, which can also be added aftermarket, can detect obstacles including other vehicles, low walls and small children. Of course, again, this should not allow a driver to become complacent when backing up.

Collision Avoidance System/Adaptive Cruise Control/ Automatic Emergency Braking: These systems override driver input or lack of it and apply braking to help avoid a frontal collision.

Vehicle Lane Departure Warning: A lane departure warning system warns the driver if the vehicle begins to stray from the lane it is in – unless a turn signal is on indicating driver intent to change lanes.

This warning can be in the form of a vibration in the steering wheel. Some systems will even act to prevent a lane departure. These systems work at least on highways and other major arterial roadways and typically use a camera or infrared detection system to monitor road markings. Some systems work in conjunction with a vehicle's cruise control to make driving less cumbersome to the driver. Other systems use differential braking instead of steering to help a driver remain in the current lane. This system only momentarily assists the driver and is not a self-driving technology.

Night Vision: Vehicle night vision typically uses the near-infrared light spectrum to enable the driver to see better in poor visibility conditions such as fog, rain or night low light conditions. It can assist in detecting vehicles, objects, pedestrians and animals in these conditions. There are active and passive systems. Passive systems detect near-infrared emissions from the source. Active systems use a front (or rear) mounted near-infrared spotlight that is invisible to the human eye to illuminate objects. The night vision display can be projected onto a vehicle's instrument display. While these systems can aid vision, they should be used only as a supplement to your normal visual scan. Staring at these displays to long may cause you to miss other critical sensory cues and could promote an accident. The best way to use them is to scan normally through the front windscreen, side windows, and mirrors, with brief glances only at the night vision display.

Parental Controls: It is no offense against teens: they are just statistically high-risk drivers. There are many, many horrible adult drivers who have been driving for a long time. But the combination of lack of experience, feeling immortal, and being on the leading edge of technological distraction is a lethal combination in young drivers. It is no secret that parents want parental controls in vehicles. Capabilities such as speed capping, position monitoring, video monitoring when passengers are in the car, disallowing radio before seatbelts are on and limiting radio volume are a few of the features available.

Driver Fatigue Monitoring: There are already many fatigue monitoring systems for vehicles using technologies ranging from physiological performance monitoring (heart rate, brain activity, etc.), to vehicle position in lane monitoring, driver eye or face tracking, and steering pattern monitoring. These systems can warn the driver if fatigue symptoms are detected. Sophisticated systems can even apply brakes to slow the vehicle if excessive fatigue is detected.

Heads-Up Displays (HUD): A Heads-Up Display system or HUD displays essential information such as speed and navigation cues in the driver's forward field of view. This information is either displayed on the windshield itself or through a separate "combiner" or transparent glass plate with certain properties. Doing so allows the driver to keep "heads up" looking at the road and traffic ahead while viewing essential information in his or her forward field-of-view. HUDs have been used in military aviation applications for quite some time and are finding their way increasingly into the commercial aviation environment. Aftermarket automobile units can easily display any vehicle and engine instrumentation information normally displayed in the vehicle by connecting to the onboard diagnostics (OBD-II) port, which all vehicles manufactured after January 1, 1996 have. Other units can connect to a vehicle's GPS or even to a navigation App on the driver's cell phone to display navigation information. Units built into the vehicle can be much more advanced, and will eventually display virtual reality information. The essence of a HUD's effectiveness in enhancing driver safety is contingent upon it reducing distraction, not adding to it. Displaying nonessential information in a HUD negates its value and just provides another excuse for distraction.

Self-Driving Cars and Fully Autonomous Vehicles: Self-driving vehicles can drive in many road conditions without driver input. This is analogous to an aircraft flying on autopilot. Pilots still must monitor the performance of the aircraft on autopilot and be prepared to take over immediately either because of autopilot limitations, or in the case of an emergency or out-of-control situation. Drivers must monitor their self-driving or autopilot mode diligently. Driving on autopilot is not an excuse for playing a video game while driving. Tesla's autopilot is an example of self-driving technology. It is important to note that self-driving and driver assist (safe distance and lane keeping for instance) are not the same. Driver assist technologies generally only assist for short periods of time.

At the other end of the spectrum is the autonomous vehicle technology that Google and other companies are developing. This is basically driverless vehicle technology. We are closer to widespread deployment of this technology than you might think. I personally feel it should be embraced as an option. There are many people who, because of disabilities, cannot drive, and may have limited access to traditional public transportation. Autonomous vehicle technology will allow them much more freedom to get around. And for the rest of us who have that desire to be productive (meaning, distracted) while getting around, this is a viable technology. This technology will also make traffic flow more efficient in conjunction with vehicle-to-vehicle communications.

Both self-driving and autonomous vehicle technologies will undoubtedly save thousands if not tens of thousands of lives each year because of accidents caused by distracted drivers. Again, though, just because your vehicle has autopilot does not mean you can keep your eyes off the road for very long. You must monitor vehicle performance just as a pilot does.

CONCLUSION

This guide has been about learning to achieve and maintain a high level of situational awareness in the driving environment. But good driving is about more than that. A good, conscientious driver will always try to have a net positive impact on other drivers and on traffic flow. When driving, periodically ask yourself this question: "If every driver did what I did, would the result improve traffic flow or hurt it."

It pays to be smart and courteous when driving. Because vehicles are controlled by human beings, traffic is the quintessential dynamic collective living organism. As in a city full of people or a hive full of bees, you are either helping the collective whole, or hurting it. This is not rocket science. It just takes a little conscience and forethought. As in life, it is not just about you. Although you cannot blindly trust in another driver you do not even know, you can be trustworthy, and predictable. You can be a good wingman.

Situational awareness can be learned. It is critical to guaranteeing safety and survivability when driving, flying, running in the park, or performing just about any "complex" activity where not having SA subjects you to lethal threats. SA is the foundation of effective decision-making. Experience does not guarantee the driver will have higher SA. As a pilot gains no experience—despite experience flying upright—in recovering from the worst aircraft upsets without proper attention and training, neither does a driver gain experience in handling road crises if continuously distracted, and if paying no attention to maintaining a high level of situational awareness. This

158

guide is a starting point. By minimizing distraction, being attentive, you the driver can learn to become a safer driver. The principles in this guide apply to myriad activities and can benefit you greatly in driving, adventure and in life. Good luck and drive safe!

Made in the USA
Coppell, TX
03 September 2021

61743878R00089